Teen Rights and Freedoms

I Bullying

Teen Rights and Freedoms

| Bullying

David Haugen, Susan Musser, and Michael Chaney
Book Editors

GREENHAVEN PRESS
A part of Gale, Cengage Learning

Farmington Hills, Mich • San Francisco • New York • Waterville, Maine
Meriden, Conn • Mason, Ohio • Chicago

Elizabeth Des Chenes, *Director, Content Strategy*
Cynthia Sanner, *Publisher*
Douglas Dentino, *Manager, New Product*

For more information, contact:
Greenhaven Press
27500 Drake Rd.
Farmington Hills, MI 48331-3535
Or you can visit our Internet site at gale.cengage.com.

For product information and technology assistance, contact us at:

Gale Customer Support, 1-800-877-4253.
For permission to use material from this text or product, submit all requests online at www.cengage.com/permissions.

Further permissions questions can be e-mailed to permissionrequest@cengage.com.

Articles in Greenhaven Press anthologies are often edited for length to meet page requirements. In addition, original titles of these works are changed to clearly present the main thesis and to explicitly indicate the author's opinion. Every effort is made to ensure the Greenhaven Press accurately reflects the original intent of the authors. Every effort has been made to trace the owners of copyrighted material.

Cover Image © O Driscoll Imaging/Shutterstock.com.

LIBRARY OF CONGRESS CATALOGING-IN-PUBLICATION DATA

Bullying / David Haugen, Susan Musser, and Michael Chaney, book editors.
    p. cm. -- (Teen rights and freedoms)
  Includes bibliographical references and index.
  ISBN 978-0-7377-6399-7 (hardcover)
  1. Bullying in schools--Law and legislation--United States. I. Haugen, David M., 1969- editor of compilation. II. Musser, Susan, editor of compilation. III. Chaney, Michael P., 1957- editor of compilation.
  KF4160.B85 2014
  344.73'0793--dc23
                                                      2014002605

Printed in the United States of America
1 2 3 4 5 6 7 18 17 16 15 14

Contents

The Pennsylvania Third Circuit Court of Appeals finds that a school district cannot be held legally responsible for preventing bullying between two students because current laws do not compel districts to protect students from harm from other students, nor have the administrators created the circumstances under which the bullying could occur.

The US Fourth Circuit Court of Appeals determines that a West Virginia school did not violate a student's First Amendment right to free speech when punishing her for harmful comments made online from her home, because these comments could increase into cyberbullying.

The circuit court judge in this case rules that a public school can be held liable for failing to put a stop to antigay bullying.

A psychologist argues that laws prohibiting antigay speech will only make antigay bullying worse, and only by engaging in open dialogue will this type of bullying—and its root causes—eventually be ended.

A gay teacher returns to the school he attended as a youth to speak to students on Diversity Day about the bullying he experienced and to provide support to those who continue to be targets of bullying.

Foreword

"In the truest sense freedom cannot be bestowed, it must be achieved."
Franklin D. Roosevelt,
September 16, 1936

The notion of children and teens having rights is a relatively recent development. Early in American history, the head of the household—nearly always the father—exercised complete control over the children in the family. Children were legally considered to be the property of their parents. Over time, this view changed, as society began to acknowledge that children have rights independent of their parents, and that the law should protect young people from exploitation. By the early twentieth century, more and more social reformers focused on the welfare of children, and over the ensuing decades advocates worked to protect them from harm in the workplace, to secure public education for all, and to guarantee fair treatment for youths in the criminal justice system. Throughout the twentieth century, rights for children and teens—and restrictions on those rights—were established by Congress and reinforced by the courts. Today's courts are still defining and clarifying the rights and freedoms of young people, sometimes expanding those rights and sometimes limiting them. Some teen rights are outside the scope of public law and remain in the realm of the family, while still others are determined by school policies.

Each volume in the Teen Rights and Freedoms series focuses on a different right or freedom and offers an anthology of key essays and articles on that right or freedom and the responsibilities that come with it. Material within each volume is drawn from a diverse selection of primary and secondary sources— journals, magazines, newspapers, nonfiction books, organization newsletters, position papers, speeches, and government documents, with a particular emphasis on Supreme Court and lower court decisions. Volumes also include first-person narratives from young people and others involved in teen rights issues, such as parents and educators. The material is selected and arranged to highlight all the major social and legal controversies relating to the right or freedom under discussion. Each selection is preceded by an introduction that provides context and background. In many cases, the essays point to the difference between adult and teen rights, and why this difference exists.

Many of the volumes cover rights guaranteed under the Bill of Rights and how these rights are interpreted and protected in regard to children and teens, including freedom of speech, freedom of the press, due process, and religious rights. The scope of the series also encompasses rights or freedoms, whether real or perceived, relating to the school environment, such as electronic devices, dress, Internet policies, and privacy. Some volumes focus on the home environment, including topics such as parental control and sexuality.

Numerous features are included in each volume of Teen Rights and Freedoms:

- An annotated **table of contents** provides a brief summary of each essay in the volume and highlights court decisions and personal narratives.
- An **introduction** specific to the volume topic gives context for the right or freedom and its impact on daily life.
- A brief **chronology** offers important dates associated with the right or freedom, including landmark court cases.
- **Primary sources**—including personal narratives and court decisions—are among the varied selections in the anthology.
- **Illustrations**—including photographs, charts, graphs, tables, statistics, and maps—are closely tied to the text and chosen to help readers understand key points or concepts.

- An annotated list of **organizations to contact** presents sources of additional information on the topic.

- A **for further reading** section offers a bibliography of books, periodical articles, and Internet sources for further research.

- A comprehensive subject **index** provides access to key people, places, events, and subjects cited in the text.

Each volume of Teen Rights and Freedoms delves deeply into the issues most relevant to the lives of teens: their own rights, freedoms, and responsibilities. With the help of this series, students and other readers can explore from many angles the evolution and current expression of rights both historic and contemporary.

Introduction

On September 10, 2013, twelve-year-old Rebecca Ann Sedwick took her own life by jumping from a tall silo at an abandoned cement works. At the Crystal Lake, Florida, middle school she attended, Sedwick had been victimized by several girls who verbally taunted her, may have physically confronted her, and allegedly terrorized her on social media sites. Sources report that the issue arose over a boyfriend, but the taunts attacked her self-image and self-worth, including threatening suggestions such as, "You should die." Sedwick's mother removed her daughter from the school, but the hate speech continued on the Internet. According to a September 16 story in the UK newspaper *Daily Mail*, her mother said of the accused offenders, "They would tell her she's ugly, stupid, nobody liked her, go kill herself." Young Sedwick fought back, insisting she would not give in to bullying, but authorities were convinced she simply was worn down by the constant attacks that lasted into the following school year. At one point, Sedwick changed one of her online screen names to "That Dead Girl" and ultimately wrote a message to a young male peer in North Carolina that read, "I'm jumping."

Police quickly rounded up cell phones and computer records from some of the fifteen girls who were accused of prompting Sedwick's rash act. Some experts, though, are not optimistic that much can be done to bring about atonement or achieve justice. Florida law gives schools, not the police, the power to punish bullying, so the reach of law enforcement in this case is limited. Even the legal aspects are not clear-cut. For a September 13 article, New Jersey lawyer and cyberbullying authority Perry Aftab told ABC News affiliate WJLA, "We've had so many suicides that are related to digital harassment. But we also have free-speech laws in this country." Sedwick's mother started a Facebook page to bring light to the tragedy and to help spread an anti-bullying message. She asserts that she was motivated by some of her daughter's diary entries, including Rebecca's chilling observation, "Every day more and more kids kill themselves because of bullying. How many lives have to be lost until people realize words do matter?"

Reports of teen suicide over bullying and harassment have made the news in recent years. The death of Phoebe Prince in a Massachusetts school district in January 2013 caught national attention and led to the creation of an anti-bullying task force and stiffer legislation in her home state. Pretrial hearings against Sedwick's alleged tormentors—who supposedly victimized her for having relationships with their boyfriends—got underway just days after her suicide. Other instances of bullying that have not pushed victims to take their own lives have also garnered headlines. Isabella Hankey, for example, utilized the newer, tougher Massachusetts law to sue the Concord-Carlisle High School and several school officials in August 2013 for taking no action against death threats and other acts of intimidation she received from classmates. The $2 million suit claims Hankey suffered a stress-related blood clot from the harassment and even accuses administrators of destroying records relating to the bullying reports. According to a CBS Boston report, Hankey's lawyer asserted, "It puts all the school administrators across the Commonwealth on notice that it's not going to be tolerated, that they need to be very proactive in preventing this type of event from happening to their students." Such newsworthy incidents and allegations have revealed the serious consequences of bullying and the incompleteness—and possible incompetence—of the systems set up to avert potential harms.

Although acts of bullying often go unreported or are attributed to childish behavior, the National Education Association (NEA) concludes that one in three American schoolchildren in grades six through ten are affected by bullying. Six out of ten witness an act of bullying every day, the NEA claims. Such acts might include name calling, stalking, physical intimidation, death threats, or any other acts of unwanted attention that interfere with the pursuit of education or daily activities. In 2012, the NEA committed to a public service campaign to bring the issue to the attention of children, parents, and teachers. Whether these types of responses will lead to a curtailment of bullying is yet to be seen. Writing in the wake of the 2011 suicide of Buffalo, New York, teenager Jamey Rodemeyer, *Huffington Post* education expert Christopher Emdin casts doubt on the usefulness of anti-bullying measures. In an October 18, 2011, opinion piece, Emdin contends that all of the counseling and assistance programs were available to Rodemeyer, and the teen did seek help. Still the tragedy occurred.

More significantly, though, Emdin insists the way in which bullies are demonized for their acts forces officials to isolate or expel these children instead of treating the problems that lead them to bully others. "The reality is that both the bully and victim are children who require equal doses of care and attention," Emdin writes, "Punishing a child like an adult only corrects an external behavior, and not the cause of it." He even argues that the severe punishments for bullies, which often come without explanation, turn the administrators into bullies, condoning—in the eyes of young offenders—the very practice that the officials wish to defame. Those who favor more immediate, exacting responses, though, believe the matter is serious enough to warrant a firm hand so that fewer victims get pushed to extreme acts. As the NEA affirms, "No student should be subjected to safety problems that can result from bullying and harassment."

The authors compiled in *Teen Rights and Freedoms: Bullying* explore this controversial issue from varying perspectives. Some explain how the issue has taken on prominence in modern society and how government has shaped laws in an effort to prevent serious consequences. Some maintain these measures are ineffective—either because the laws are shortsighted or overprotective—while others believe they are only part of a more comprehensive solution to an issue that is far more detrimental than many care to admit. Mixed in with these analyses are first-person narratives of those who have suffered at the hands of bullies or have parented a child who was victimized. Together, the commentators in this anthology seek to make teens aware of their rights as victims and of the larger issues that influence social policy designed to confront the problem of bullying.

Chronology

1973
Psychology professor Dan Olweus begins researching bullying among schoolchildren in Norway and publishes the first large-scale report on the issue. In 1983, Norwegian elementary and secondary schools adopt the Olweus Bullying Prevention Program to counteract suicides and other harms related to bullying. In the mid-1990s, the program is adopted in US schools.

July 1996
In *Nabozny v. Podlesny*, a Seventh Circuit Court judge rules that a gay student harassed at school could sue his principal and school board under Title IX protections. The subsequent successful suit was the first of its kind in US legal history.

March 1999
Georgia enacts the first anti-bullying legislation in response to the beating of a thirteen-year-old boy at an Atlanta school bus stop. The law provides for anti-bullying education in schools.

April 1999
At Columbine High School in Colorado, Eric Harris and Dylan Klebold plan and execute a massacre that claims the lives of twelve students and one teacher. Two dozen other students are injured in the attack that involves automatic weapons and ex-

plosives. Both Harris and Klebold were victims of bullying, and some experts suggest there is a causal link between bullying and the rash of school shootings that occur in the wake of Columbine.

December 1999

In *Davis v. Monroe County Board of Education*, the US Supreme Court determines that school boards may be held liable for damages in cases in which school officials do not act in response to harassment charges under the Title IX discrimination law.

October 2003

When thirteen-year-old Ryan Halligan commits suicide after being taunted by classmates in person and on the Internet, his father launches a campaign to end bullying in Vermont schools. The state enacts such legislation in 2004, and other states begin taking up the issue.

June 2008

Representatives Linda Sanchez and Kenny Hulshof propose a federal law that would criminalize cyberbullying. No such law has passed US Congress as of late 2013.

July 2008

High school student Jesse Logan takes her own life after classmates taunt her over sexually explicit images she once texted to an ex-boyfriend (who subsequently spread them to peers). The tragedy prompts federal lawmakers to introduce a bill calling for "sexting" education in schools.

August 2008

California becomes the first state to pass legislation to allow school districts to discipline students who engage in cyberbullying.

October 2009

President Barack Obama signs the Matthew Shepard and James Byrd Jr. Hate Crimes Prevention Act, a measure added to the National Defense Authorization Act for 2010. The law expands the definition of hate crimes to protect individuals against violence based on gender, sexual orientation, gender identity, or disability. The act is named for Matthew Shepard, a gay University of Wyoming student who was beaten to death in 1998, and James Byrd Jr., an African American man murdered in a racially motivated attack in 1998.

September 2010

Rutgers University student Tyler Clementi commits suicide after a roommate broadcasts video over the Internet of Clementi having a romantic encounter with another male student in their dorm room. The roommate, Dharun Ravi, and another student are charged with invasion of privacy.

November 2010

The hit television show *Glee* confronts the issue of bullying when a gay character is harassed at school by an athlete (who has trouble contending with his own homosexuality).

September 2011   New Jersey enacts one of the toughest anti-bullying laws, calling on schools to address all claims and file reports and findings with the state.

November 2011   Recording artist Lady Gaga establishes the Born This Way Foundation to promote self-esteem, acceptance, and tolerance. The organization relies on local supporters to speak out against bullying and other acts of hate.

December 2012   North Carolina criminalizes the bullying of teachers by students.

2013   Forty-nine state governments possess some form of anti-bullying statutes for their schools. Only Montana does not.

June 2013   In *Morrow v. Balaski*, the Pennsylvania Third Circuit Court of Appeals contends that a school district does not have a constitutional duty under the Fourteenth Amendment to protect students from harassment at school.

> "Student bullying is one of the most
> frequently reported discipline issues
> in schools."

Bullying and the Response of Schools: An Overview

Scott LaFee

In the viewpoint that follows, Scott LaFee provides a broad overview of the varying responses to bullying that can be observed in school districts across the country. A carefully considered response to the problem is necessary, according to the school staff and leaders LaFee interviewed, because bullying affects so many students and the consequences can be so devastating, in some cases leading an individual to commit suicide. The author shows the seriousness with which school staff and legislators have approached this problem and presents the many policies that have been crafted at the local, state, and federal levels to attempt to stop bullying. However, disagreement as to whether a single policy or set of guidelines can be implemented in all schools persists, according to LaFee, and anti-bullying responses must be made at a local level by individual school district administrators and staff. Scott LaFee is a journalist who has written for the San Diego Union-Tribune *for more than twenty-five years.*

Scott LaFee, "The Political and Cultural Complications of Bullying," *School Administrator Magazine,* April 2012, published by AASA, The School Superintendents Association. Reprinted with permission.

Nine days into Scott Martzloff's first year as superintendent of the Williamsville Central School District, a suburban community just outside Buffalo, N.Y., a high school freshman named Jamey Rodemeyer committed suicide.

"I became superintendent in July 2011," recalls Martzloff. "Two months later, on Sept. 18, Jamey died. I was still meeting people in the district, still shaking hands and learning names. I obviously didn't know Jamey."

But in the days and months that followed, Martzloff—and the world—would come to know at least parts of Jamey's story well. Within 24 hours of his death, Rodemeyer's family, friends and others were talking about his life and death in newspapers, on radio and on national TV. It was alleged the openly gay 14-year-old had been bullied and harassed by classmates for years, at school and online. Jamey had chronicled his troubles in chat rooms, tweets and YouTube videos, frequently encouraging other gay teens to fight back, especially against thoughts of suicide.

Rodemeyer's death garnered immediate headlines, the latest example in a seeming epidemic of student suicides spawned by bullying, often connected to issues of sexual orientation or gender identity. Celebrities like Lady Gaga rallied around Jamey's story and cause. New state legislation against bullying was proposed in his name.

Schools Can React to Bullying Even If the Law Does Not

In his western New York school district of 10,400 students, Martzloff found himself caught in a media-driven maelstrom of questions, concerns and criticism. Did bullying really drive Jamey to suicide? Could it have been prevented? What did school officials know? What did they do?

Local police investigated and uncovered at least five episodes of on-campus harassment of Rodemeyer. However, the investigators concluded that school officials were not aware of the specific incidents until after his death. Authorities ultimately closed the case without filing any criminal charges. Jamey's suicide, they said, appeared to be the consequence of multiple factors, not just bullying.

Still, based on information provided by the police, Martzloff suspended several students for bullying or harassing Rodemeyer. Their identities and the terms of their suspensions were not announced.

"Whether a student is gay or not, no one deserves to be harassed. Not for any reason," Martzloff says. "Everybody has a right to come to school and be accepted for who they are. After Jamey's death, I held parent forums at all 13 schools in the district. One of the things I asked people was how many of them had ever been bullied. Generally, about half would raise their hands. Bullying is not a contemporary problem. It has always been there."

Laws Fail to Define and Punish Bullying

Student bullying is one of the most frequently reported discipline issues in schools. According to the 2010 Indicators of School Crime and Safety, produced by the federal departments of education and justice, 21 percent of elementary schools, 43 percent of middle schools and 22 percent of high schools report significant problems with bullying.

Members of minority groups are the typical targets. These days, that most often means students whose sexual orientation or gender identity attracts the ire of others. In a school climate survey of 7,261 middle and high school students conducted by the advocacy group Gay Lesbian Straight Education Network [GLSEN], almost all lesbian, gay, bi-sexual or transgender students reported having been harassed in school. Two-thirds said they felt unsafe on campus because of their sexual orientation.

At last count [as of April 2012], 48 states have anti-bullying laws on their books, most mandating some kind of response or action from school districts. The two exceptions are Montana and

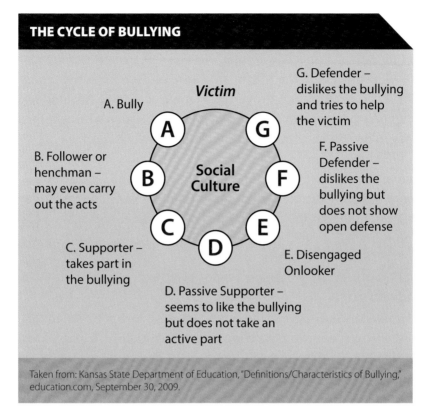

THE CYCLE OF BULLYING

Victim

A. Bully

G. Defender – dislikes the bullying and tries to help the victim

B. Follower or henchman – may even carry out the acts

Social Culture

F. Passive Defender – dislikes the bullying but does not show open defense

C. Supporter – takes part in the bullying

E. Disengaged Onlooker

D. Passive Supporter – seems to like the bullying but does not take an active part

Taken from: Kansas State Department of Education, "Definitions/Characteristics of Bullying," education.com, September 30, 2009.

South Dakota. But clarity and direction from state legislators is hardly a given. The subject of bullying is fraught with political, social and cultural complications, and school districts often must find their own way through the inevitable, fractious controversies.

Consider the case of Michigan. Last November [2011], the state senate passed a controversial bill requiring school districts to adopt anti-bullying policies. However, the bill was excoriated by critics who cited its exemptions for offensive statements or acts based on a "sincerely held religious belief or moral conviction of a school employee, school volunteer, pupil or a pupil's parent or guardian."

A leading critic of the legislative bill was Michael Flanagan, the state superintendent of public instruction, who said: "I cannot imagine any real moral conviction or religious teaching that says it is acceptable to inflict pain, humiliation and suffering on another person, especially a child."

Lawmakers in the Michigan House of Representatives eventually removed the controversial exemptions, and a final bill was signed into law in December by Gov. Rick Snyder, who acknowledged he had been bullied throughout his school years.

The new Michigan law requires every school district to enact an anti-bullying policy, but it does not proscribe specific behaviors, much to the consternation of groups like GLSEN, who say it's essential that the specific bases of harassment be defined and prohibited.

Schools Worry About Federal Laws' Overreach

New Jersey may have the toughest anti-bullying policy in the nation. The state's Anti-Bullying Bill of Rights, which passed last year [2011], was prompted by the 2010 death of an 18-year-old Rutgers University freshman who jumped to his death from the George Washington Bridge into the Hudson River after a roommate posted a secretly filmed sexual encounter of him on the Internet. The law contains 18 pages of required components that every school district must follow. Among them:

- Increased staff training and tight deadlines (a one-day turnaround) for investigating alleged incidents, on campus or off;
- Designated anti-bullying specialists on each campus and a districtwide coordinator;
- Twice-a-year reports to the state department of education, which will post compliance scores;
- A penalty of lost professional licenses for failure to comply.

The federal government also has stepped up its interest. In 2010, the U.S. Department of Education's Office of Civil Rights [OCR] mailed a "Dear Colleague Letter" to districts nationwide.

The letter's intent, OCR officials said at the time, was to clarify the relationship between bullying and discriminatory harassment under civil rights law. More specifically, it was meant to underscore the federal government's position that unmitigated bullying may be a violation of students' civil rights and that schools were legally obliged to both stop it and prevent it.

"Once a school knows or reasonably should know of possible student-on-student harassment," the OCR stated, "it must take immediate and appropriate action to investigate or otherwise determine what occurred."

If harassment has occurred, the OCR said school officials must take "prompt and effective steps" to end the harassment, eliminate any hostile environment and prevent its recurrence. These steps must be taken regardless of whether a student complains of harassment or asks for official action.

The letter has prompted concerns about overreach, unintended consequences and the ability of schools to adequately implement and sustain required programs. "Our fear is that, absent clarification, the department's expansive reading of the law will invite misguided litigation that needlessly drains precious school resources and creates adversarial school climates that distract schools from their educational missions," wrote General Counsel Francisco M. Negron Jr. of the National School Boards Association in a letter to the Department of Education.

But education officials dismiss those concerns, noting that the Dear Colleague Letter simply reiterates existing laws and policies and provides new examples of how to combat bullying. And the OCR has followed up its words with actions.

School Districts Are Held Responsible for Failing to Stop Bullying

Seth Walsh was a 13-year-old middle school student in the Tehachapi Unified School District, a sprawling, 4,900-student rural district southeast of Bakersfield, Calif., who committed suicide just one month before the OCR letter was sent.

Walsh, who was gay, had long complained of frequent bullying by classmates, who mocked his appearance and mannerisms. On Sept. 19, 2010, he attempted to hang himself from a backyard tree. He died from associated injuries nine days later. A suicide note to his family read, in part: "Please put my body in burial and visit my used body. And make sure to make the school feel like **** for bringing you this sorrow."

After investigating, the OCR concluded that district staff failed to stop or prevent harassment of Walsh for more than two years. District officials initially denied knowledge of Walsh's harassment, but later agreed to revise their policies and regulations regarding sexual and gender-based harassment, to hire a consultant to conduct mandatory training sessions for all students, teachers and staff, and to conduct regular climate surveys.

A similar story is still playing out in the Anoka-Hennepin School District, northwest of Minneapolis and Saint Paul. The 40,000-student district is the largest in Minnesota and, for the last year at least, one of the bigger players in the bullying debate.

Two years ago [2010], Anoka-Hennepin board of education members passed a controversial policy that said if the subject of sexual orientation came up in class, teachers were obliged to take

A vigil is held to remember Jamey Rodemeyer outside Williamsville North High School. The fourteen-year-old was bullied for years before he committed suicide in September 2001.
© Buffalo News, Sharon Cantillon/AP Images.

a neutral stance. A parent sued the school district alleging two teachers had harassed her son because they thought he was gay. The district eventually settled the lawsuit for $25,000. Between 2009 and 2010, Minnesota Public Radio reported that seven students in the district committed suicide, some of whom were gay and alleged victims of bullying.

School officials deny the connection between harassment and the suicides, but the federal departments of education and justice are investigating. Dennis Carlson, the Anoka-Hennepin superintendent, declined to talk about the situation, citing ongoing federal mediation.

Schools Worry Anti-Bullying Laws Infringe on Local Autonomy

Often missing in the anti-bullying directives from state and federal entities is how exactly school districts are supposed to implement them, particularly if the mandates are unfunded—as they often are.

Richard Bozza, executive director of the New Jersey Association of School Administrators, supports the intent of his state's tough anti-bullying law. "School leaders cannot and should not avoid the issue," he says.

On the other hand, he adds, "The law takes away the autonomy of school personnel to deal most effectively with very minor issues since an investigation and formal reporting are required. The law places the burden of addressing bullying solely on the school system. This is an issue which requires the support of parents, civic and community leaders and clergy to adequately address the larger society issue."

Nonetheless, school districts across the country are taking action. The Fort Worth Independent School District has expanded its anti-bullying policy to protect nontraditional "gender identity and expression" among students. It's reportedly the first district in Texas to do so. Broward County Public Schools in Florida has done the same.

The process isn't necessarily easy. For example, Montana does not have a statewide anti-bullying policy, but in the summer of 2010, Helena Public Schools officials, led by veteran superintendent Bruce K. Messinger, unveiled new, frank guidelines for teaching about sexuality and tolerance, part of a broader effort to address the issues of bullying and harassment.

The guidelines covered all age groups, progressing from 1st graders learning that "human beings can love people of the same gender" to 5th graders being taught that sexual intercourse takes multiple forms.

Community response was seriously divided, and particularly sharp among local conservative and religious groups, which complained the proposed materials were too explicit and promoted official acceptance of homosexuality.

After several months of roiling debate, a divided Helena school board adopted a revised plan that excised most of the original language for more vague descriptions. Parents also were granted the option of removing their children from lessons they found objectionable.

Messinger left the district a year later to take the superintendent's job in Boulder, Colo. He was replaced by Keith Meyer, an assistant superintendent for 14 years and a 30-year district employee. Meyer had been preparing to retire, but agreed to be interim superintendent for at least a year.

Schools Can Mandate Anti-Bullying Curriculum

When asked about the issue of bullying in Helena, Meyer is circumspect. He says the controversy was fueled more by poor communications and a flawed process than by the actual content of the guidelines.

"Communication had broken down between the school board, the superintendent and the community on this topic," Meyer says. "We discovered you cannot simply tell people what they should know and believe. You have to listen to what they're saying as well. We're trying to rebuild that trust and I feel good about it."

Meyer says the district's current anti-bullying policy, recommended by the Montana School Boards Association, is "aggressive" but could be improved. (A district survey found half of the students between the ages of 12 and 14 said they had been bullied.) The district has hired a consultant and devoted additional staff development days to the topic.

"'Expect respect' is our mantra this year," Meyer says. "We want to improve relations between all people—students, staff, kids, adults. I've been doing a lot of listening and what I hear is that people really want to help, if you ask them to help. We're doing that."

Other districts have grappled more forcefully with the issue of bullying. The Alameda Unified School District in northern California introduced new tolerance lessons in 2009 after teachers observed elementary-age students using gay slurs and teasing children with gay or lesbian parents. One new lesson included using a children's book about two male penguins bonding and raising a chick.

Some parents in the 8,900-student district in the San Francisco Bay region demanded the right to remove their children from lessons they found objectionable. Superintendent Kirsten Vital refused, telling reporters at the time: "This is really anti-bullying curriculum. Not health or sex ed. It's not appropriate necessarily to have an opt-out provision." The parents sued the district but lost.

Lawsuit or not, the district has worked hard over the years to define and refine its anti-bullying curriculum. "We have provided professional development, crafted school and district policies, enacted instructional leadership practices to guide and shape those efforts," she says. "This plan of action was vetted and adopted by the Alameda board, by staff and community in interactive community engagement efforts over time to answer questions and educate the public writ large to issues of bullying and our need to educate students about our legal and moral imperative of safeguarding the rights of all people."

Communication Is the Key to Stopping Bullying

Few would dispute Vital's argument, but the debate over when and how school districts address the problem of bullying remains broadly unresolved. Ken Trump, president of the National School Safety and Security Services, a Cleveland-based consulting firm, says the issue has become "highly politicized." He asserts it is grossly exaggerated by special interest groups with their own agendas.

Conversely, Peter DeWitt, principal of Poestenkill Elementary School in Averill Park, N.Y., and author of the upcoming book *Dignity for All*, complains most school districts have not done enough.

"I'm a little tired of school districts that choose to bury their head in the sand on this issue," says DeWitt, who blogs on the subject of bullying. "They have students who are at risk of dropping out of school, experimenting with drugs, alcohol and unsafe sex and are considering death by suicide. If schools do not include language to help these students or ignore the issues, they are part of the problem and are allowing the bullying to occur. By not standing up against it, they are condoning bullying behavior."

Back in Williamsville, Superintendent Martzloff has come to a similar but simpler conclusion. The district operated multiple wellness and anti-bullying programs before the death of Jamey Rodemeyer. They remain in place and have been beefed up where possible, according to Martzloff.

But one of the most important lessons he's learned is simply that districts must create and promote an atmosphere of trust between children and adults. "Kids need to know they can go to a grownup—a teacher, a principal, someone on staff—when they have a problem, whether it's bullying or something else," Martzloff says.

"That confidence has to extend to local parents and the community, too," he adds. "In our case, Jamey's death produced a lot of national coverage, and some of it was very slanted. But if local parents and the community believe in what you're doing as a school district and as educators, then things will generally turn out OK."

> *"Deliberate indifference to known acts of harassment . . . amounts to an intentional violation of Title IX."*

School Boards Can Be Punished for Failing to Protect Students from Harassment

US Supreme Court's Decision

Sandra Day O'Connor

In the case of Davis v. Monroe County Board of Education (1999), the family of fifth grader LaShonda Davis sued the Monroe County Board of Education in 1994 for failing to take disciplinary action against a male classmate who continually sexually harassed the young girl. After a series of appeals, the US Supreme Court was left to determine whether a school could be held liable under Title IX of the Education Amendments of 1972 for failing to intervene when one student harasses another. The viewpoint that follows presents the majority opinion of the court, written by Justice Sandra Day O'Connor, who argues that a school's continued inaction to stop the harassment of one student by another constitutes a decision by the school not to act, which in turn makes the school liable for the consequences that result from the continued harassment. For

Sandra Day O'Connor, *Davis v. Monroe County Board of Education*, US Supreme Court, May 24, 1999.

LaShonda Davis, the consequences included falling grades and thoughts of suicide. Because the impact of the harassment was severe and the school took no steps to punish the boy or stop the harassment, O'Connor ruled the student and her family were entitled to monetary compensation from the school board. Sandra Day O'Connor served as a Supreme Court justice from 1981 to 2006; she was the first woman to become a Supreme Court judge.

Title IX [of the Education Amendments of 1972] provides, with certain exceptions not at issue here, that

> [n]o person in the United States shall, on the basis of sex, be excluded from participation in, be denied the benefits of, or be subjected to discrimination under any education program or activity receiving Federal financial assistance.

Congress authorized an administrative enforcement scheme for Title IX. Federal departments or agencies with the authority to provide financial assistance are entrusted to promulgate rules, regulations, and orders to enforce the objectives of § 1681, see § 1682, and these departments or agencies may rely on "any . . . means authorized by law," including the termination of funding, to give effect to the statute's restrictions.

There is no dispute here that the Board is a recipient of federal education funding for Title IX purposes. Nor do respondents support an argument that student-on-student harassment cannot rise to the level of "discrimination" for purposes of Title IX. Rather, at issue here is the question whether a recipient of federal education funding may be liable for damages under Title IX under any circumstances for discrimination in the form of student-on-student sexual harassment.

Schools Cannot Receive Title IX Funding If They Permit Discrimination

Petitioner urges that Title IX's plain language compels the conclusion that the statute is intended to bar recipients of federal

Attorney Verna Williams (speaking) and the parents of LaShonda Davis meet reporters outside the US Supreme Court on January 12, 1999. The Davis family sued the Monroe County Board of Education for failing to discipline a male classmate who sexually harassed their daughter. The Supreme Court ruled in the family's favor and established that schools can be held liable for the harassment of a student. © Ron Edmonds/file/AP Images.

funding from permitting this form of discrimination in their programs or activities. She emphasizes that the statute prohibits a student from being "*subjected to discrimination* under any education program or activity receiving Federal financial assistance." (emphasis added). It is Title IX's "unmistakable focus on the benefited class," *Cannon v. University of Chicago* (1979), rather than the perpetrator, that, in petitioner's view, compels the conclusion that the statute works to protect students from the discriminatory misconduct of their peers.

Here, however, we are asked to do more than define the scope of the behavior that Title IX proscribes. We must determine whether a district's failure to respond to student-on-student harassment in its schools can support a private suit for money damages. This Court has indeed recognized an implied private right of action under Title IX, and we have held that money damages are available in such suits. Because we have repeatedly treated Title IX as legislation enacted pursuant to Congress' authority under the Spending Clause, however, private damages actions are available only where recipients of federal funding had adequate notice that they could be liable for the conduct at issue. When Congress acts pursuant to its spending power, it generates legislation "much in the nature of a contract: in return for federal funds, the States agree to comply with federally imposed conditions." *Pennhurst State School and Hospital v. Halderman* (1981). In interpreting language in spending legislation, we thus "insis[t] that Congress speak with a clear voice," recognizing that "[t]here can, of course, be no knowing acceptance [of the terms of the putative contract] if a State is unaware of the conditions [imposed by the legislation] or is unable to ascertain what is expected of it."

Schools Can Only Be Held Responsible for Their Own Actions

Invoking *Pennhurst*, respondents urge that Title IX provides no notice that recipients of federal educational funds could be liable in damages for harm arising from student-on-student harassment. Respondents contend, specifically, that the statute only proscribes misconduct by grant recipients, not third parties. Respondents argue, moreover, that it would be contrary to the very purpose of Spending Clause legislation to impose liability on a funding recipient for the misconduct of third parties, over whom recipients exercise little control.

We agree with respondents that a recipient of federal funds may be liable in damages under Title IX only for its own misconduct. The recipient itself must "exclud[e] [persons] from participation in, ... den[y] [persons] the benefits of, or ... subjec[t] [persons] to discrimination under" its "program[s] or activit[ies]" in order to be liable under Title IX. The Government's enforcement power may only be exercised against the funding recipient, and we have not extended damages liability under Title IX to parties outside the scope of this power.

Failure to Act Constitutes a Punishable Action

We disagree with respondents' assertion, however, that petitioner seeks to hold the Board liable for G. F.'s [a fifth-grade classmate] actions instead of its own. Here, petitioner attempts to hold the Board liable for its *own* decision to remain idle in the face of known student-on-student harassment in its schools. In *Gebser* [*v. Lago Vista Independent School District* (1998)], we concluded that a recipient of federal education funds may be liable in damages under Title IX where it is deliberately indifferent to known acts of sexual harassment by a teacher. In that case, a teacher had entered into a sexual relationship with an eighth-grade student, and the student sought damages under Title IX for the teacher's misconduct. We recognized that the scope of liability in private damages actions under Title IX is circumscribed by *Pennhurst's* requirement that funding recipients have notice of their potential liability. Invoking *Pennhurst, Guardians Assn.* [*v. Civil Serv. Comm'n of New York City* (1983)], and *Franklin* [*v. Gwinnett County Public Schools* (1992)], in *Gebser* we once again required "that 'the receiving entity of federal funds [have] notice that it will be liable for a monetary award'" before subjecting it to damages liability. ...

We consider here whether the misconduct identified in *Gebser*—deliberate indifference to known acts of harassment— amounts to an intentional violation of Title IX, capable of supporting a private damages action, when the harasser is a student

Bullying Is a Recently Recognized Problem

Prior to the 1970s, American society did not consider bullying to be a significant problem. At the time, many people had the attitude that students should toughen up, or that bullying was an inevitable part of life. In the early 1970s, Dan Olweus, a psychology professor at the University of Bergen in Norway, completed the first large-scale study of school bullying. In 1978, Olweus published the study in the United States in the book *Aggression in the Schools: Bullies and Whipping Boys*. This book helped to raise awareness about the problem of bullying in the schools. In the 1980s, Olweus conducted the "first systematic intervention study" that discussed the benefits of a bullying prevention program. Since this study, educators have conducted other large-scale intervention programs in the schools. In 1993, Olweus wrote the book *Bullying at School: What We Know and What We Can Do*. During the 1990s, this book was considered to be the world's leading authority on bullying. Olweus's research has played an important role in increasing awareness about the problem of bullying.

Farley Anderson, "Pacifism in a Dog-Eat-Dog World: Potential Solutions to School Bullying,"
Mercer Law Review, *Spring 2013.*

rather than a teacher. We conclude that, in certain limited circumstances, it does. As an initial matter, in *Gebser* we expressly rejected the use of agency principles in the Title IX context, noting the textual differences between Title IX and Title VII. Additionally, the regulatory scheme surrounding Title IX has long provided funding recipients with notice that they may be liable for their failure to respond to the discriminatory acts of certain nonagents. The Department of Education requires recipients to monitor third parties for discrimination in specified circumstances and to refrain from particular forms of interaction with outside entities that are known to discriminate.

The common law, too, has put schools on notice that they may be held responsible under state law for their failure to protect students from the tortious acts of third parties. In fact, state courts routinely uphold claims alleging that schools have been negligent in failing to protect their students from the torts of their peers.

School Liability Depends on Its Control Over the Harassment

This is not to say that the identity of the harasser is irrelevant. On the contrary, both the "deliberate indifference" standard and the language of Title IX narrowly circumscribe the set of parties whose known acts of sexual harassment can trigger some duty to respond on the part of funding recipients. Deliberate indifference makes sense as a theory of direct liability under Title IX only where the funding recipient has some control over the alleged harassment. A recipient cannot be directly liable for its indifference where it lacks the authority to take remedial action.

The language of Title IX itself—particularly when viewed in conjunction with the requirement that the recipient have notice of Title IX's prohibitions to be liable for damages—also cabins the range of misconduct that the statute proscribes. The statute's plain language confines the scope of prohibited conduct based on the recipient's degree of control over the harasser and the environment in which the harassment occurs. If a funding recipient does not engage in harassment directly, it may not be liable for damages unless its deliberate indifference "subject[s]" its students to harassment. That is, the deliberate indifference must, at a minimum, "cause [students] to undergo" harassment or "make them liable or vulnerable" to it. . . . Moreover, because the harassment must occur "under" "the operations of" a funding recipient, the harassment must take place in a context subject to the school district's control. . . .

Where, as here, the misconduct occurs during school hours and on school grounds—the bulk of G. F.'s misconduct, in fact, took place in the classroom—the misconduct is taking place "under" an "operation" of the funding recipient. In these circumstances, the recipient retains substantial control over the context in which the harassment occurs. More importantly, however, in this setting the Board exercises significant control over the harasser. . . .

Schools Retain the Ability to Discipline Students as They See Fit

We stress that our conclusion here—that recipients may be liable for their deliberate indifference to known acts of peer sexual harassment—does not mean that recipients can avoid liability only by purging their schools of actionable peer harassment or that administrators must engage in particular disciplinary action. We thus disagree with respondents' contention that, if Title IX provides a cause of action for student-on-student harassment, "nothing short of expulsion of every student accused of misconduct involving sexual overtones would protect school systems from liability or damages." Likewise, the dissent erroneously imagines that victims of peer harassment now have a Title IX right to make particular remedial demands. In fact, as we have previously noted, courts should refrain from second-guessing the disciplinary decisions made by school administrators.

School administrators will continue to enjoy the flexibility they require so long as funding recipients are deemed "deliberately indifferent" to acts of student-on-student harassment only where the recipient's response to the harassment or lack thereof is clearly unreasonable in light of the known circumstances. The dissent consistently mischaracterizes this standard to require funding recipients to "remedy" peer harassment, and to "ensur[e] that . . . students conform their conduct to" certain rules. Title IX imposes no such requirements. On the contrary, the recipient must merely respond to known peer harassment in a manner that is not clearly unreasonable. This is not a mere "reasonable-ness" standard, as the dissent assumes. In an appropriate case, there is no reason why courts, on a motion to dismiss, for summary judgment, or for a directed verdict, could not identify a response as not "clearly unreasonable" as a matter of law.

Like the dissent, we acknowledge that school administrators shoulder substantial burdens as a result of legal constraints on their disciplinary authority. To the extent that these restrictions arise from federal statutes, Congress can review these burdens with attention to the difficult position in which such legislation may place our Nation's schools. We believe, however, that the standard set out here is sufficiently flexible to account both for the level of disciplinary authority available to the school and for the potential liability arising from certain forms of disciplinary action. A university might not, for example, be expected to exercise the same degree of control over its students that a grade school would enjoy, and it would be entirely reasonable for a school to refrain from a form of disciplinary action that would expose it to constitutional or statutory claims. . . .

Students Must Be Protected from Harassment

Applying this standard to the facts at issue here, we conclude that the Eleventh Circuit erred in dismissing petitioner's complaint. Petitioner alleges that her daughter was the victim of repeated acts of sexual harassment by G. F. over a 5-month period, and there are allegations in support of the conclusion that G. F.'s misconduct was severe, pervasive, and objectively offensive. The harassment was not only verbal; it included numerous acts of objectively offensive touching, and, indeed, G. F. ultimately pleaded guilty to criminal sexual misconduct. Moreover, the complaint alleges that there were multiple victims who were sufficiently disturbed by G. F.'s misconduct to seek an audience with the school principal. Further, petitioner contends that the harassment had a concrete, negative effect on her daughter's ability to receive an education. The complaint also suggests that petitioner may be able to show both actual knowledge and deliberate indifference on the part of the Board, which made no effort whatsoever either to investigate or to put an end to the harassment.

On this complaint, we cannot say "beyond doubt that [petitioner] can prove no set of facts in support of [her] claim which would entitle [her] to relief." *Conley v. Gibson* (1957). Accordingly, the judgment of the United States Court of Appeals for the Eleventh Circuit is reversed, and the case is remanded for further proceedings consistent with this opinion.

> *"Bias, bullying and harassment currently stand between too many youth and this essential opportunity [to get an education]."*

Your Take: Why We Need Anti-Bullying Legislation

Eliza Byard and Sharon J. Lettman

In the following viewpoint, Eliza Byard and Sharon J. Lettman argue that schools need to do more to protect students from bullying. They cite a national survey conducted by Harris Interactive to make the case that students feel safer in schools where the entire staff takes a proactive approach to bullying. The authors assert that staff training and comprehensive anti-bullying policies are key to making students feel safe, which is crucial to a good education. Eliza Byard is the executive director of the Gay, Lesbian and Straight Education Network. Sharon J. Lettman is the executive director of the National Black Justice Coalition.

One year ago, a black boy from Massachusetts took his own life over bullying. A white girl's recent suicide in a nearby town reminds us why we must act now to end the hate.

Last week, Northwestern Massachusetts District Attorney Elizabeth Scheibel took action to reverse a terrible trend plaguing families and schools across the country: the rise of "bullicide." Scheibel filed charges against nine high school students at South Hadley High School as a result of the death of Phoebe Prince. Prince, a 15-year-old Irish immigrant, hanged herself after being relentlessly taunted by her classmates. She was harassed online, physically attacked at school and repeatedly called "slut" and "whore" to her face. Her mother claims teachers were aware of her daughter's abuse, but did nothing.

Coincidentally, these charges come as Sirdeaner Walker marks the one-year anniversary of the death of her 11-year-old son, Carl Joseph Walker-Hoover. Last April, Carl, like Phoebe, hanged himself. At his Springfield, Mass., middle school—less than 10 miles from South Hadley High School—Carl was called the "f-word" and other anti-gay slurs on a daily basis. It didn't matter that he did not identify as gay, Carl's peers tormented him until he could no longer bear it. Sirdeaner reported the problem to school officials. They told her that teasing was ordinary social interaction that would eventually work itself out over time.

Two young people—one white girl, one black boy—whose short lives ended in suicide. Both linked to the same culprits: Bullying and schools' inability to deal effectively with this nationwide crisis.

Bullying Is a Big Problem in Schools Today

According to *From Teasing to Torment*, a national survey conducted by Harris Interactive and the Gay, Lesbian and Straight Education Network (GLSEN) of 3,400 students ages 13–18, two-thirds (65 percent) reported that they have been verbally or physically harassed or assaulted during the past year because of their perceived or actual appearance, gender, sexual orientation, gender expression, race/ethnicity, disability or religion. The survey also found that 39 percent of students were frequently harassed based on their appearance and 33 percent because they are or are perceived to be lesbian, gay or bisexual.

As we mourn the terrible losses of Phoebe and Carl, we must recommit ourselves to a societal effort to end bullying, once and for all. The specifically sexist and homophobic bullying that Phoebe and Carl experienced is all too common. And evidence shows that school officials often do not act in the face of such unacceptable behavior. Only about a third of students who reported incidents of victimization to school personnel said that staff effectively addressed the problem, according to GLSEN's 2007 National School Climate Survey. More disturbing, nearly two-thirds of students heard homophobic remarks from school personnel.

This must stop.

Schools Must Take a Proactive Approach Toward Bullying

Schools that take action to address bullying do see results, if they implement two crucial interventions. We need anti-bullying policies that specifically address the myriad forms of societal bias that can fuel some of the most egregious bullying cases, including race and ethnicity, gender, religious affiliations, sexual orientation, gender identity and expression, [and] ability, among other distinguishing characteristics found in our diverse society.

There must be staff training to promote timely and even-handed responses to bullying incidents. Comprehensive anti-bullying policies help ensure that the students most at risk are afforded equal access to an education, free from fear and intimidation. Students from schools with a comprehensive policy are 50 percent more likely to feel very safe at school (54 percent vs. 36 percent). Students without such a policy are three times more likely to skip a class because they feel uncomfortable or unsafe (16 percent vs. 5 percent).

We must demand that our schools be places that prepare youth for life in our diverse society, and that the federal govern-

Sirdeaner Walker (left) who lost her eleven-year-old son to suicide, addresses an audience during an anti-bullying bill signing ceremony at the State House in Boston, Massachusetts, in 2010. © Steven Senne/AP Images.

ment, currently so active on many other education issues, lead the way on this one as well. To honor Carl's memory, Sirdeaner Walker has become an outspoken advocate for the Safe Schools Improvement Act, federal legislation that would make effective anti-bullying policies mandatory in nearly every school in the United States. This is not about criminalizing bullying, or jailing individual offenders as may happen in Massachusetts, but about preventing bullying by building school communities that foster respect for all.

Last month, Sirdeaner Walker spoke at a press conference in Massachusetts to call for effective and comprehensive anti-bullying legislation in response to the Prince tragedy and the loss of her son, Carl. She reminded legislators of what is truly at stake in this fight:

STATE ANTI-BULLYING LAWS AND POLICIES

- Laws Only
- Policy Only
- Both Laws and Policy

Taken from: Stopbullying.gov, 2010.

In the immortal words of U.S. Supreme Court Chief Justice Earl Warren, "it is doubtful that any child may reasonably be expected to succeed in life if he is denied the opportunity of an education." Bias, bullying and harassment currently stand between too many youth and this essential opportunity.

My son was denied a lifetime of opportunities. I am here to make sure that no other child has to endure what my son went through, and that no other family suffers as mine has.

Now is the time for effective, proactive, educationally appropriate responses to bullying, before another child ends his or her own life. Now is the time to speak to your member of Congress about passing the Safe Schools Improvement Act. Now is the time to speak up for those who can no longer speak for themselves, and to guarantee all of our children a lifetime of opportunity.

4

| "*Anti-bullying laws have turned out to be empowering tools for educrats.*"

Anti-Bullying Laws Suppress Free Speech

J.D. Tuccille

As bullying has become an increased focus of legislators and the media, the laws enacted to combat it have become more intrusive on free speech rights, according to J.D. Tuccille in the following viewpoint. The problem is exemplified in the author's view by the case of two high school seniors in New Jersey whose diplomas were withheld by their school as a result of perceived bullying in their graduation speeches. While the students in this example eventually did receive their diplomas, Tuccille maintains that this case resulted from New Jersey's severe anti-bullying laws, which have been identified by free speech advocates as detrimental to First Amendment rights. These laws have been drawn up in response to the overstatement of the bullying, according to Reason *editor Nick Gillespie, when in fact incidents of bullying in schools actually have decreased in recent years. J.D. Tuccille is a journalist and managing editor of* Reason.com.

Yet another pack of school officials has discovered that the current panic over "bullying" provides a handy pretext for punishing mouthy students who irritate them. In Middletown, New Jersey—hometown of our own Nick Gillespie [editor of Reason.com and Reason TV]—graduating Middletown High School South senior class presidents Eric Dominach and Mike Sebastiano were denied their diplomas and warned that some mild chop-busting in their graduation speech may have violated anti-bullying guidelines and warranted a formal investigation. The two are raising a ruckus and demanding apologies, but they're not the only people to be bullied by anti-bullying laws.

Students Have Been Denied Diplomas Due to Supposed Bullying

From the *Asbury Park Press*:

> Dominach and Sebastiano say Principal Patrick Rinella asked them before graduation to delete parts of the speech, including a reference to the school's "50 other vice principals"—a joke about the school having multiple vice principals. The seniors also were asked to delete a gibe about the difficulty they had trying to get into the National Honor Society, despite stellar grades.
>
> But the teens restored those and other comments at the last minute and kept in jokes about classmates they say the district had never attempted to censor. The speech also included a comment about a fellow student who taught them how to fight and another who "never shut up." That student, they say, had been voted "Most Talkative" in school-sanctioned class elections.
>
> When Dominach and Sebastiano went to the high school to pick up their diplomas June 18 with the rest of their classmates, they were told the documents would be withheld. The next day the families were told all students and staff named would be interviewed to determine whether they felt bullied, and whether charges might be filed, the families said, though no one had filed a complaint.

"Our speech didn't justify that outcome. We knew our speech didn't offend anyone," Sebastiano said. "We thought it was unfair."

"I was very surprised," said Eric Dominach, an honor student who will major in engineering at Rutgers University in fall. "We wanted the speech to leave a memorable mark on our four years and just bring enjoyment to all the students who graduated. . . . (District officials) just didn't want it to be funny, I guess, or for us to state obvious facts about our school and the things we had to go through."

The district held the diplomas until June 20, just before a Board of Education meeting at which parents and students had been planning to protest.

Anti-Bullying Laws Have Been Ruled Unconstitutional

New Jersey's recently adopted anti-bullying law . . . had already drawn the ire of free-speech advocates. The Foundation for Individual Rights in Education [FIRE] noted that:

> by prohibiting speech that "has the effect of insulting or demeaning any student or group of students" in such a way as to "substantially disrupt—or interfere—with the orderly operation of the institution," New Jersey has in effect sanctioned the "heckler's veto." If the College Republicans were to stage a disruptive sit-in because the College Democrats had harshly criticized them for being Republicans, New Jersey's law would subject the Democrats to punishment for the Republicans' disruption. In other words, New Jersey has incentivized overreaction to any perceived insult, since the "victim's" disruption of the orderly operation of the school automatically shifts the blame to the speaker.

What FIRE didn't say is that the law also incentivizes speech-averse officials to go *hunting* for the hecklers' veto, by seeking out somebody—anybody—who can claim to be offended. That's

Good Anti-Bullying Legislation Provides Protection from Bullies and Guarantees Free Speech

Bullying in schools is a difficult problem that calls for immediate attention. But because of its natural implications on the First Amendment rights of students, solving the problem requires a very delicate balance from schools and legislators nationwide.

So, is New Jersey's harsh, new anti-bullying statute a model statute for the states? Not quite. Although critics of the statute worry that it imposes too many responsibilities—which include inherent costs—on teachers and the community, the statute is actually successful in providing a strong focus on anti-bullying education. In this particular aspect of the statute, the increased regulation is actually a positive change. But New Jersey's legislation is not successful in other key aspects, namely its direct off-campus legislation, which infringes on students' First Amendment rights not only because it extends beyond the school grounds, but also because it does so according to schools officials' discretion. . . .

Because the First Amendment rights of students are vital rights, statutes, especially New Jersey's, must be tailored to eliminate the vagueness and overbreadth problems. Fortunately, even though most states' legislation have First Amendment complications at present, these states need only tailor a small part of their laws to make them First Amendment approved. Once states tailor their statutes and decide to take a more preventative approach, students across the United States will have two of their freedoms restored: safety from bullies and freedom of speech.

Lindsay Nash, "New Jersey's Anti-bullying Fix: A Solution or the Creation of an Even Greater First Amendment Problem?," Brigham Young University Law Review, *2012.*

Anti-bullying activists walk outside the New Jersey State House in 2010 as lawmakers hold hearings on a bill that would toughen New Jersey's anti-bullying laws. Free speech advocates believe these laws are detrimental to First Amendment rights. © Mel Evans/AP Images.

usually not too challenging a task, so it's a minor miracle that Dominach and Sebastiano weren't ultimately confronted with thin-skinned "victims."

New Jersey's law was actually ruled unconstitutional in January—as a violation of state provisions regarding unfunded mandates, rather than free speech protections. Lawmakers promptly responded by funding the muzzle-friendly monstrosity. That's a shame, because the state law not only defines a remarkably vague range of speech as harassment and bullying, but it also makes such behavior punishable "whether it be a single incident or a series of incidents," and both "in school and off school premises" meaning it's pretty damned easy to run afoul of the statute, if somebody wants you to.

In using an anti-bullying law as a cudgel against students who direct unwelcome criticism their way, Middletown officials join colleagues elsewhere, including San Francisco. Anti-bullying laws have turned out to be empowering tools for educrats.

The Bullying Problem Has Been Exaggerated

But they're really the only ones being empowered. Writing in the *Wall Street Journal, Reason's* Nick Gillespie writes that, while bullying sucks, the modern bullying panic is a load of hysterical crap:

> Despite the rare and tragic cases that rightly command our attention and outrage, the data show that things are, in fact, getting better for kids. When it comes to school violence, the numbers are particularly encouraging. According to the National Center for Education Statistics, between 1995 and 2009, the percentage of students who reported "being afraid of attack or harm at school" declined to 4% from 12%. Over the same period, the victimization rate per 1,000 students declined fivefold.

Dominach and Sebastiano appear to be winning their battle in Middletown, since they're now demanding an apology from school officials. But speech-suppressing anti-bullying laws remain in place in New Jersey and elsewhere.

> "We need not, however, determine whether any of these incidents constitute bullying. Rather, this case involves a failure of supervision and of dissemination of information."

Schools Can Be Sued for Failing to Protect Students from Bullying

State Court of Appeals Ruling

Andy D. Bennett

When Misty Phillips's son Jacob Gentry entered the seventh grade, she worked with the staff at the White House Heritage School to ensure that the teachers and school officials were aware of her son's difficulty interacting with other students and handling stress in the classroom. The school was informed of her son's condition after evaluation and diagnosis by a clinical psychologist, and plans were made to help him succeed in school. However, after he was involved in an altercation with another student that left him legally blind in one eye, Phillips sued the school district for failing to prevent the bullying incident from occurring. In the Tennessee State Court of Appeals ruling that follows, Judge Andy D. Bennett rules that the school failed to take action, based on the known information about

Andy D. Bennett, *Misty Phillips on behalf of her minor son Jacob Gentry v. Robertson County Board of Education*, State Court of Appeals Ruling, September 11, 2012.

Jacob's condition, to protect the student and thus could be held liable for the injuries he incurred. Bennett based his ruling on the facts that the school should have foreseen the incident based on Jacob's past reaction to stress and interaction with students, failed to provide the appropriate supervision to ensure no harm came to Jacob, and did not equip his teachers with adequate information about his condition. Due to these facts, the judge found the school could be sued for failing to prevent the incident from occurring. Andy D. Bennett has served as a Tennessee State Court of Appeals judge since his appointment in 2007.

On May 17, 2006, there was a physical altercation between Jacob and another child, W.K. When this incident occurred, the teacher, Amanda Knipfer (now Pass), was out of the room. W.K. hit Jacob in the eye with a book during the altercation, and Jacob sustained serious injuries to his left eye that necessitated four surgeries and left him legally blind in that eye.

Ms. Phillips [Jacob's mother] filed this negligence suit against the Robertson County Board of Education, the superintendent, two principals, and a teacher in May 2007. . . .

The school learned of Jacob's diagnosis of Asperger's at least by the November 10, 2005 support team meeting. Ms. Phillips and Jacob both testified that they reported numerous instances of bullying and teasing to school officials and teachers. According to the testimony of Ms. Phillips, Principal Baggett, and Ms. Pedigo [the school psychologist], Ms. Phillips "was constantly reporting such incidents [of bullying and teasing] to school officials and demanding that something be done." School officials denied observing the alleged bullying and teasing and asserted that Jacob's problems with other students were "mutual" or "a function of Jacob's inability to understand and interact appropriately with his peers." Ms. Pedigo "acknowledged that it is not uncommon for children with Asperger's to be considered 'bully magnets.'" School officials acknowledged that Jacob had "meltdowns" at school; during these episodes, he could not think rationally and was often unable to express to teachers or administrators what had happened.

The trial court determined that it was not necessary to resolve all of the conflicts in the testimony regarding whether bullying occurred and whether the school responded appropriately. It summarized the essential facts to be as follows:

> [T]he school system was aware that Jacob had Asperger's and the characteristics or indications that Jacob would exhibit as a result. These would include such things as appearing isolated, having difficulty reading social cues, having difficulty getting along with peers, and having problems socially. The school was aware that Jacob could exhibit meltdowns or other inappropriate behavior and actually observed and documented such behavior. The school was aware that he could be a "bully magnet." Whether or not the school observed Jacob being bullied or was able to verify all [of] Jacob's accounts of bullying, it was nonetheless aware of his complaints and the validity of some of them.

Awareness of Potential for Bullying Can Result in Negligent Behavior

Principal Baggett acknowledged that some of Jacob's complaints of bullying were corroborated and resulted in action against the other students involved. He did not know if the contents of [clinical psychologist] Dr. [Arie L.] Nettles's April 2006 letter were communicated to Jacob's teachers. The school system had a policy that students be under the supervision of school personnel at all times of the school day.

Ms. Knipfer began teaching at White House in the spring of 2006. She did not recall having problems with Jacob in class. Although she had heard about Jacob's Asperger's diagnosis during "water fountain talk" with other teachers, she did not recall being officially advised of any issues involving Jacob. The only accommodation for Jacob she knew about was the preferential seating. Ms. Knipfer did not recall seeing any communication from [Dr.

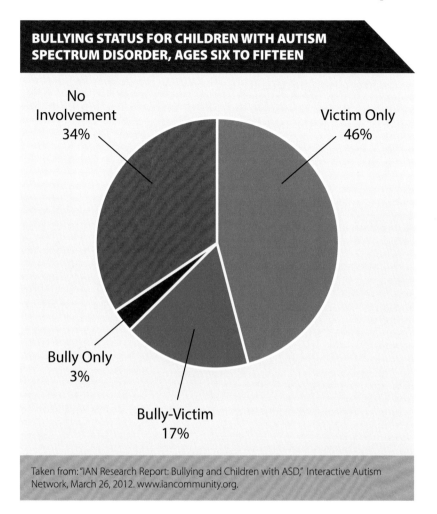

BULLYING STATUS FOR CHILDREN WITH AUTISM SPECTRUM DISORDER, AGES SIX TO FIFTEEN

No Involvement 34%

Victim Only 46%

Bully Only 3%

Bully-Victim 17%

Taken from: "IAN Research Report: Bullying and Children with ASD," Interactive Autism Network, March 26, 2012. www.iancommunity.org.

Nettles at] Vanderbilt about Jacob's special needs or reviewing Jacob's IEP [Individual Education Program]. Ms. Knipfer knew about the school policy regarding supervision of students. On the day in question, however, she had an emergency and did not remember whether she had asked another teacher to supervise.

Ms. Thompson, the assistant principal, testified that she knew about complaints regarding other students bullying Jacob. She never saw Dr. Nettles's April 2006 letter. In her testimony, Ms. Thompson acknowledged that, at her deposition, she had stated that she believed she had sent W.K. to guidance for bullying. Ms. Thompson had sent some students through a bullying program because of interactions with Jacob.

In his testimony, W.K. stated that there was no teacher in the classroom when he and Jacob had the altercation at issue. He did not believe that the incident would have escalated as it did if a teacher had been in the room.

Both Ms. Phillips and Jacob testified that "W.K. had been identified as one of the students bullying Jacob in the many conversations and meetings that occurred between Ms. Phillips and/ or Jacob and school officials." Principal Baggett, Ms. Thompson, and Ms. Pedigo, however, "testified that W.K. was never specifically identified as a student bullying or mistreating Jacob."

Based upon the testimony, the court found "that Jacob was a victim of bullying and that the school was on notice that the bullying was occurring." The court further found:

> Ms. Knipfer did not review Jacob's IEP, was not made aware of Jacob's special needs and circumstances by school officials, was never shown any of the information contained in Dr. Nettles['s] initial evaluation or April letter and did not follow school policy or the instructions of the principal and assistant principal concerning supervision of her classroom. . . . Further, the court finds that the failure of the other school officials to appropriately [disseminate] information concerning Jacob to those needing to know was also negligence. Had Ms. Knipfer known of the issues involving Jacob she may have made extra effort to be certain that the classroom was supervised by someone during her absence or sent Jacob out of the classroom as she left. The principal testified that Jacob should never have been left alone in a classroom without a teacher present because of his conditions and his complaints of bullying, yet this critical information was not given to Ms. Knipfer.

The trial court concluded that the incident in which Jacob was injured "was foreseeable; that it occurred as the result of the negligence of the Defendant and that the negligence of the

Defendant was the proximate cause of the accident or injury." In a final order entered on January 13, 2012, the court entered judgment in favor of the plaintiff in the amount of $300,000.00.

A Conflict Must Be Foreseeable for a Party to Be Negligent

On appeal, the County argues that the physical conflict between Jacob and W.K. was not foreseeable and that the acts of the school employees were not negligent.

In a cause of action for negligence, a plaintiff must establish five elements: a duty of care owed by the defendant to the plaintiff, breach by the defendant of that duty of care, injury or loss, cause in fact, and proximate or legal cause. Schools districts "are not expected to be insurers of the safety of students while they are at school." *Roberts v. Robertson Cnty. Bd. of Educ.* (Tenn. Ct. App. 1985). School districts do, however, have a duty to safeguard students while at school from "reasonably foreseeable dangerous conditions including the dangerous acts of fellow students." *Id.* The question of whether there has been a breach of the duty of care is an issue for the trier of fact. Foreseeability, an essential component of proximate (or legal) cause, is an issue of fact, and the trial court's findings regarding foreseeability are, therefore, entitled to a presumption of correctness.

The County argues that the physical conflict between Jacob and W.K. was not foreseeable so as to make the County's acts the proximate or legal cause of his injuries.

Foreseeability is an essential part of proving proximate (or legal) cause. If the plaintiff's injury "could not have been reasonably foreseen or anticipated," there is no proximate (or legal) cause [as stated in *Roberts*]. *Id.* There is no requirement that the defendant foresee the exact manner in which the injury took place; rather, [the *Roberts* ruling found] it must be determined that the defendant "could foresee, or through the exercise of reasonable diligence should have foreseen, the general manner in which the injury occurred."

In Misty Phillips, on behalf of her minor son Jacob Gentry v. Robertson County Board of Education *(2012), the Tennessee State Court of Appeals ruled that schools can be held liable for failing to protect students from bullying.* © Istockphoto.com/Steve Debenport.

Foreseeability Is Not Dependent on the History of the Participants

The County argues that foreseeability must be based upon the history of the participants in a particular incident and that there is no evidence of prior incidents involving Jacob and W.K. As the plaintiff points out, the trial court did hear evidence supporting a prior history of incidents involving W.K. and Jacob. Ms. Phillips testified that W.K. was one of the six boys she identified by name to the school as bullying Jacob. Jacob and Ms. Phillips both testified that they told school officials or teachers about specific incidents involving W.K. shortly after they occurred. In its factual findings, the trial court noted that Ms. Thompson, in deposition testimony, stated that "she believed she had sent W.K. to guidance for bullying."

The County argues that the evidence does not support the trial court's finding about Ms. Thompson's testimony. . . .

Based upon all of the testimony, we conclude that the evidence does not preponderate against the trial court's finding that Ms. Thompson "believed she had sent W.K. to guidance for bullying," especially since this determination hinged in part on the trial court's evaluation of the witness's credibility. The trial court specifically noted the contrary testimony of other school officials that W.K. "was never specifically identified as a student bullying or mistreating Jacob."

The County also emphasizes that W.K.'s name does not appear in any of the school records related to Jacob. However, school officials admitted at trial that school records did not document everything that occurred at support team meetings or in communications between school employees and parents. Principal Baggett and Ms. Thompson testified that they did not keep records or notes from their meetings with Jacob or his mother. Moreover, the fact that Jacob did not list W.K. on his preferred seating list for Ms. Knipfer's class is not inconsistent with his allegations of being teased and bullied by W.K. because, for that class, Jacob only listed students he wanted to sit near, not those he did not want to sit near.

Furthermore, we do not accept the County's premise that foreseeability must be based on a history of previous incidents involving the same students. . . .

A Student's Special Conditions Could Suggest Foreseeability

In the present case, . . . the school was aware of prior incidents of bullying or teasing involving Jacob, and there was some evidence that W.K. was one of the bullying students identified to the school. Moreover, . . . Jacob had special needs that were known to the school. As the trial court found, "the school system was aware that Jacob had Asperger's and the characteristics or indications that Jacob would exhibit as a result." The school knew that Jacob had difficulty reading social cues and getting along with peers and that he had "meltdowns." Even if the school was not aware of any previous physical altercations involving Jacob or W.K., as emphasized by the County, Jacob's social limitations and tendency to react inappropriately made a physical confrontation foreseeable.

The trial court's conclusions of law include the following:

> Given what the Defendant knew about Jacob, his limitations, his perceptions, his complaints and those of his mother, and the actions they had taken against other students after investigating Jacob's complaint, it was certainly foreseeable that other incidents in which Jacob would be abused or perceive himself to be abused would occur. It was also foreseeable that Jacob would react in an inappropriate manner.

In light of Jacob's special circumstances and the school's knowledge of his problems and history, we cannot say that the evidence preponderates against the trial court's finding of foreseeability.

Students with Special Needs Should Not Be Left Unattended

The County also argues that its actions were not negligent—i.e., that the school did not breach the duty of care owed to Jacob. The trial court found the County negligent as follows:

> Ms. Knipfer was negligent in failing to follow the school board's policy and the instructions of the principal and assistant principal with regard to leaving students in the classroom unattended. . . . The principal and other school officials were negligent in failing to properly advise Ms. Knipfer of Jacob's condition and in failing to properly follow through with regards to the accommodations they had agreed to make for Jacob.

The evidence does not preponderate against the trial court's determination that the County breached its duty of care.

With respect to the teacher leaving the class unattended, the County argues that leaving a class of seventh graders unsupervised for five minutes is not negligent. Under the circumstances of this case, however, we must disagree. Principal Baggett testified that it was school policy not to leave children unsupervised and that, if a teacher had to leave the classroom, he or she was to ask another teacher to "keep an eye" on the class. Principal Baggett further testified that, in light of Jacob's condition and his complaints about bullying, he should not have been left in the room without a teacher present. In light of what the school system knew about Jacob and his complaints of bullying, the evidence does not preponderate against the trial court's conclusion that Ms. Knipfer was negligent when she left him unsupervised in a classroom with a group of middle school students lined up for dismissal.

Information to Help Prevent Bullying Must Be Shared with All Teachers

As to the second ground for negligence (failure to disseminate information), the County argues that the IEP process "was not designed to serve the purpose of addressing issues like autism, Asperger's, or social problems." The salient point, however, is that the school system failed to disseminate, through the IEP process or otherwise, important information about Jacob's Asperger's and his problems with bullying. Ms. Knipfer started in the middle of the year. She testified that, through informal conversations with other teachers, she learned that Jacob had been diagnosed with Asperger's and that he was allowed to have preferential seating. According to Ms. Knipfer's testimony, she was not given individualized information about the nature of Jacob's Asperger's diagnosis, how the condition affected him, or what might trigger symptoms. She was not aware of the information in the psychologist's letter, sent in April 2006, that children with Asperger's were often teased and bullied. She was not aware of any other accommodations (other than preferential seating) applicable to Jacob. Furthermore, Ms. Knipfer was not advised that Jacob and his mother had complained of bullying by W.K. Ms. Knipfer testified that, had she known about Jacob's limitations, she would have been much more likely to make sure someone was watching her classroom.

The evidence does not preponderate against the trial court's finding that the school system was negligent in failing to properly advise Ms. Knipfer about Jacob's condition.

Finally, we note that the County disagrees with the plaintiff's use of the term "bullying," asserting that the incidents reported by Jacob and his mother reflect the kind of teasing and "goofing" engaged in by typical middle school kids. We need not, however, determine whether any of these incidents constitute bullying. Rather, this case involves a failure of supervision and of dissemination of information. Given what it knew about Jacob's developmental limitations, including his inability to react appropriately to social cues and his tendency to have meltdowns, the school board should have foreseen that he could be injured by another student when left unsupervised.

> "We need to wake up and teach our kids
> about respect, guide them in ways to
> always see others, and figure out how
> to actively pour good into society."

The Mother of a Bullied Student Argues That Parents Must Take Action to Stop Bullying

Personal Narrative

Lori Twichell

In the viewpoint that follows, Lori Twichell recounts her daughter's experiences with bullying as an elementary school student and the school's inability to respond to the torments of her teacher and other students. The author makes the argument that parents are best positioned to stop bullying. Twichell asserts that after her daughter reported incidents of playground bullying by another student to her teacher, her teacher began to engage in bullying of her own to toughen up the young girl. When the author's daughter approached the school's administration to try to remedy the situation, her teacher was reprimanded for her actions, but only limited disciplinary action could be taken, and the bullying just worsened. While the school attempted to address the situation and put an end to the bullying, school policies allowed only limited options for recourse and eventually Twichell had to remove her daughter from the school. Twichell uses this example to highlight the fact that schools, even with the best intentions, cannot always stop bullying, and parents must take action to protect their children when bullied. Lori Twichell is a professional writer who owns the marketing company Beyond the Buzz Marketing and homeschools her three children with her husband, an Air Force veteran.

Recently, I posted an article [on the blog LoriTwichell.com] about bullying. I asked if it had changed or if we, as a society, had changed. I think that this is a really complex answer and I don't believe that it can be addressed with any measure of value in a series of blog entries. Still, this is my platform and bullying hurts my heart in a personal way, so this is my attempt.

Schools Often Have Few Options to Address Bullying

My family has dealt with severe and powerful bullying on more than one occasion. A few years ago, a little girl at my daughter's school decided that she didn't like my daughter. It happens all the time and unfortunately, it's something we all must get used to. It's going to happen at some point or another. But this went above and beyond normal dislike. On a daily basis, she would find ways to tell my daughter that she was a pointless human being. On the playground, for example, she would send boys out to chase my daughter and "assassinate" her so the world would be a better place. This is when I really started to see how much the school could and couldn't do on her behalf. The girl who was bullying my daughter wasn't actually in her class. This tied a lot of hands in the administration. They weren't sure how to handle it since simply removing the girls from each other's company wasn't an option. According to the teachers, the only "games" on the playground involved tag. They can't always regulate what kids say to each other or how they do it.

My daughter took her issues to her teacher—who promptly informed her that she needed to suck it up. Life was hard and she should ignore those other kids. However, the daily torment got worse and worse. The teacher, now understanding the issue, decided that she needed to toughen my daughter up. So she started a campaign of her own. She'd single my daughter out in class to toughen her up. Make her answer questions in front of the other students. Call her "out" regularly for even the most minor infraction. As my daughter began to crumble, she realized it wasn't

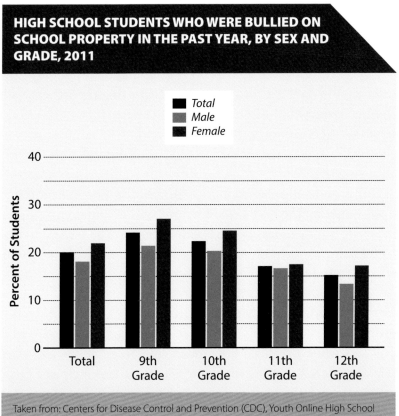

HIGH SCHOOL STUDENTS WHO WERE BULLIED ON SCHOOL PROPERTY IN THE PAST YEAR, BY SEX AND GRADE, 2011

Taken from: Centers for Disease Control and Prevention (CDC), Youth Online High School Risk Behavior Survey, 2012.

good and at the age of 11, she went to the principal on her own. The principal was appalled at the realization that this was going on and immediately stepped in.

This is where things got sticky. See, there's very little the school can actually do to help a kid being bullied. Their hands are tied with policies and rules from higher up. They went through their standards and practices—all of which were to bring both kids into the office and force them to try to be friends. They attempted to mitigate the situation by making the kids like each other. That won't work. Kids aren't stupid. They know what answers teachers (and parents) are looking for. They simply need to give the "Sunday School Answers" and then there's nothing else the school can do.

The bullying continued. No one had a clue what to do. And there was a new element. The teacher. My daughter's teacher was unhappy with being called out by the administration. She was not pleased to have a "mark" on her reputation. Suddenly, my child who had all A's all year long with glowing reports, started coming home with nasty notes about her behavior, constant critiques of everything she did, and nothing my daughter did was good enough. Literally. The torment from the bully was nothing compared to the teacher's behavior. And even though the principal and administration recognized this, there was nothing they could do. The teacher had tenure. My daughter couldn't be moved to another class because class sizes were all packed to the hilt already. The school's solution? My 11 year old went to school every day and worked in the office with the staff.

Only Parents Can Stand Up for Their Kids

This was when I realized how much rules, regulations and zero tolerance policies had affected our schools. The principal, a huge number of the teachers and many of the staff at the school saw what was happening. They all loved my daughter and understood how bad it was, but there was little to nothing they were permitted to do about it. Their hands were tied. It really underscored the core issue for me and this was why I decided to let go of public school for my family. No matter how much we liked the staff, administration and teachers (for the most part!) at my daughter's school, there was little they could do to keep her safe enough to get her education.

To answer the question, bullying has changed, but so have we. It's become more vitriolic and it's more intense than it was 20 years ago. Kids aren't just calling names—they're literally threatening lives. A friend of mine made national headlines when her son threatened suicide due to a similar sort of bullying. Again, the school was unable to do anything to help him due to zero tolerance policies. The bullies understand the rules and are able to bend them to fit their needs. The schools are terrified to step outside the lines and do anything that might cause headlines or a lawsuit. So no one stands up against bad behavior.

We have changed too. The advent of the Internet has created a society that's rife with disrespectful people, anger, and vitriol that spews everywhere. Just look at the hatred and anger in recent elections! We need to wake up and teach our kids about respect, guide them in ways to always see others, and figure out how to actively pour good into society. That is the only way that bullying will ever be dealt with in a proper manner. And we must do this with and for our kids because no one else is going to stand up for them like we (their parents) will.

> *"The increasing prevalence of the kind of bullying alleged here has generated considerable discussion and legislative action. Nonetheless, 'the Constitution does not provide judicial remedies for every social . . . ill.'"*

School Districts Cannot Be Held Liable for Bullying That Occurs Between Students

Circuit Court Ruling

Theodore Alexander McKee

During the winter of the 2007–2008 school year, Brittany and Emily Morrow, sisters and students at Blackhawk High School in Pennsylvania, began to face bullying in the form of threats, physical violence, and online bullying from fellow student Shaquana Anderson. The school took disciplinary action to stop the bullying, and the girls' parents involved the local police, leading to probation for Anderson. However, the attacks continued, and after the school failed to guarantee the sisters' safety, they changed schools to avoid further confrontation. The Morrows sued the school district, claiming Brittany's and Emily's Fourteenth Amendment rights were violated by the lack of protection offered by the school. In the following Third Circuit Court ruling, Judge Theodore Alexander McKee finds that the Due Process Clause does not require a state to protect

Theodore Alexander McKee, *Morrow v. Balaski*, US Circuit Court, June 5, 2013.

individuals from harm that may occur at the hands of others; the amendment only protects individuals from harm inflicted by the state. McKee bases this opinion on the constitutional reading that mandatory-attendance public school policies do not rob students of their freedom in the same way as involuntary incarceration, thus relieving the school of the duty to protect students from other students. He continues that school control over students is not great enough to warrant the protection offered by the Fourteenth Amendment. Theodore Alexander McKee is the chief judge of the US Court of Appeals for the Third Circuit, a position he has held since 2010.

To state a claim under 42 U.S.C. § 1983, a plaintiff must allege a person acting under color of state law engaged in conduct that violated a right protected by the Constitution or laws of the United States. *Nicini v. Morra* (3d Cir. 2000). Accordingly, "[t]he first step in evaluating a section 1983 claim is to 'identify the exact contours of the underlying right said to have been violated' and to [then] determine 'whether the plaintiff has alleged a deprivation of a constitutional right at all.'" *Id.* (quoting *Cnty. of Sacramento v. Lewis* (1998)).

Due Process Does Not Hold States Responsible for All Harm Experienced by Individuals

As we noted at the outset, the Morrows' § 1983 claim rests on the Due Process Clause of the Fourteenth Amendment. The Due Process Clause provides that a state shall not "deprive any person of life, liberty, or property, without due process of law." U.S. Const. amend. XIV, § 1. The Morrows invoke the substantive component of due process, which "protects individual liberty against 'certain government actions regardless of the fairness of the procedures used to implement them.'" *Collins v. City of Harker Heights* (1992) (quoting *Daniels v. Williams* (1986)). Specifically, the Morrows allege that school officials violated a liberty interest by failing to protect Emily and Brittany from the threats and assaults inflicted by fellow students.

Like the District Court, we are sympathetic to the Morrows' plight. Brittany and Emily were verbally, physically and—no doubt—emotionally tormented by a fellow student who was adjudicated delinquent based on her actions against the Morrow sisters. When the Morrows requested that the Defendants do something to protect Brittany and Emily from the persistent harassment and bullying, school officials responded by suggesting that the Morrows consider moving to a different school rather than removing the bully from the school.

We therefore certainly understand why the Morrows would conclude that the school's response to the abuse inflicted on their daughters was unfair and unjust. Nevertheless, our adjudication of the Morrows' claims must be governed by Supreme Court precedent. As we shall explain, it is also guided by authoritative Supreme Court *dicta*.

The Supreme Court has long established that "[a]s a general matter, . . . a State's failure to protect an individual against private violence simply does not constitute a violation of the Due Process Clause." *DeShaney v. Winnebago Cnty. Dep't of Social Servs.* (1989). The Due Process Clause forbids the state *itself* from depriving "individuals of life, liberty, or property without 'due process of law,' but its language cannot fairly be extended to impose an affirmative obligation on the State to ensure that those interests do not come to harm through other means." *Id.* at 195. . . .

Public School Attendance Does Not Deprive Students of Liberty

As the Court instructed in *DeShaney,* an affirmative duty to protect may arise out of certain "special relationships" between the state and particular individuals. The Supreme Court has found that the relationship between the state and its incarcerated or involuntarily committed citizens is the kind of "special relationship" that creates an affirmative duty upon the state to provide adequate medical care to incarcerated prisoners, and to ensure the "reasonable safety" of involuntarily committed mental patients, *Estelle* [*v. Gamble* (1976)] and *Youngberg* [*v. Romeo* (1982)], "[t]aken together . . . stand . . . for the proposition that when the State takes a person into its custody and holds him there against his will, the Constitution imposes upon it a corresponding duty to assume some responsibility for his safety and general well-being." *DeShaney*, 489 U.S. at 199–200.

It is clear from the decision in *DeShaney* that the state's constitutional "duty to protect arises not from the State's knowledge of the individual's predicament or from its expressions of intent to help him, but from the limitation which it has imposed on his freedom to act on his own behalf." *Id.* at 200. In other words, "it is the State's affirmative act of restraining the individual's freedom to act on his own behalf—through incarceration, institutionalization, *or other similar restraint of personal liberty*—which is the 'deprivation of liberty' triggering the protections of the Due Process Clause, not its failure to act to protect his liberty interests against harms inflicted by other means." *Id.* (emphasis added).

A minor child attending public school most certainly does not have the freedom of action or independence of an adult. Nevertheless, the Supreme Court has not had occasion to specifically decide whether that is sufficient to create a special relationship between public schools and their students under the Due Process Clause. We have, however, previously considered the application of the special relationship doctrine in the public school context. In *D.R. v. Middle Bucks Area Vocational Technical School* (3d Cir. 1992), a sixteen-year-old hearing and communication-impaired student ("D.R.") and a seventeen-year-old classmate ("L.H.") alleged that several male students physically, verbally, and sexually assaulted them during a graphic arts class during the school day over a period of several months. The male students forced them into the classroom's unisex bathroom or darkroom and physically abused and sexually molested the

In Morrow v. Balaski *(2013), the US Court of Appeals for the Third Circuit ruled that schools cannot be held liable for bullying between students.* © Istockphoto.com/Robert Churchill.

plaintiffs multiple times per week. A student teacher was present in the classroom when the abuses occurred. Although D.R. did not claim to have informed her of the situation, D.R. alleged that the teacher either heard the assaults or should have heard them. L.H. alleged that she complained to the school's assistant director about the boys' conduct, but he took no action.

Although we recognized the horrific nature of the allegations, we nevertheless held that "the school defendants' authority over D.R. during the school day cannot be said to create the type of physical custody necessary to bring it within the special relationship noted in *DeShaney*." *Id.* at 1372. We rejected the plaintiffs' argument that Pennsylvania's compulsory school attendance laws and the school's exercise of *in loco parentis* [legal term meaning "in place of a parent"] authority over its students so restrain the students' liberty that they can be considered to have been in state "custody" during school hours for Fourteenth Amendment purposes. Our conclusion was largely informed by the fact that "parents remain the primary caretakers, despite their [children's] presence in school." *Id* at 1371. We explained that "[t]he *Estelle-Youngberg* type custody referred to by the Court in *DeShaney* . . . is to be sharply contrasted with D.R.'s situation." *Id.* Although the doctrine of *in loco parentis* certainly cloaks public schools with some authority over school children, . . . that control, without more, is not analogous to the state's authority over an incarcerated prisoner or an individual who has been involuntarily committed to a mental facility.

Nonetheless, when we decided *Middle Bucks*, the Supreme Court's jurisprudence allowed room to debate this issue because the Court had not enumerated the parameters of the control or custody required for the creation of a special relationship under the Fourteenth Amendment. Accordingly, in a compelling dissent to the *Middle Bucks* majority, then-Chief Judge Sloviter argued for a "functional" approach to "custody":

> I believe that we are free to decide . . . that the state compulsion that students attend school, the status of most students as minors whose judgment is not fully mature, the discretion extended by the state to schools to control student behavior, and the pervasive control exercised by the schools over their students during the period of time they are in school, combine to create the type of special relationship which imposes a constitutional duty on the schools to protect the liberty interests of students while they are in the state's functional custody. . . .

In addition, every other Circuit Court of Appeals that has considered this issue in a precedential opinion has rejected the argument that a special relationship generally exists between public schools and their students. . . .

School Control Over Students Has Not Increased

Accordingly, the Supreme Court's *dictum* in *Vernonia [School District 47J v. Acton* (1995)] as well as the consensus from our sister Circuit Courts of Appeals both reinforce our conclusion that public schools, as a general matter, do not have a *constitutional* duty to protect students from private actors. We know of nothing that has occurred in the twenty years since we decided *Middle Bucks* that would undermine this conclusion. We therefore find the dissent's assertion here that "factual developments since *Middle Bucks* have further undercut its rationale," unpersuasive. The first two examples our dissenting colleagues offer of "schools exercising greater control over students" include the use of technology tracking student movement to ensure they are in class and the monitoring of social media activity by students. Such examples merely illustrate new precautionary measures some schools have undertaken in response to emerging technology. It is difficult to see how such measures constitute limitations on a student's "freedom to act on his own behalf," that are so severely restrictive as to equate public school students with prisoners or those who are involuntarily committed to secure mental institutions.

Similarly, a school's exercise of authority to lock classrooms in the wake of tragedies such as those that have occurred in Newtown, Connecticut and [Columbine], Colorado, may be a relevant factor in determining whether a special relationship or a state-created danger exists in those specific cases. However, the fact that *certain* schools may resort to such restrictions does not advance our inquiry here or allow us to conclude that the facts alleged in the Complaint are sufficient to give rise to a special relationship or a state created danger. . . .

Compulsory Attendance Does Not Create a Special Situation Requiring Protection for Students

As discussed above, we cannot hold that a special relationship arose from compulsory school attendance laws and the concomitant *in loco parentis* authority and discretion that schools necessarily exercise over students, or the school's failure to do more to protect Brittany and Emily, without ignoring the analysis in *DeShaney*, and the "considered dicta" in *Vernonia School District*.

In arguing to the contrary, our dissenting colleagues exaggerate the extent of a school's control over its students. Judge Fuentes insists that "[t]he State's authority over children while they are in school extends beyond their well-being and *is nearly absolute.*" (emphasis added). However, the mere fact that a school can require uniforms, or prescribe certain behavior while students are in school, does not suggest a special relationship at all. Rather, such commonly accepted authority over student conduct is inherent in the nature of the relationship of public schools and their pupils. They do not suggest that a concomitant constitutional duty to protect students necessarily arises from that authority.

Significantly, our dissenting colleagues do not purport to argue that compulsory attendance laws and the school's authority over students are themselves sufficient to satisfy the limited exception carved out in *DeShaney.* Thus, the dissent attempts to characterize the specific circumstances of this case as so extraordinary and compelling that a constitutional duty to protect arose under *DeShaney.* We are not persuaded.

School Policies Did Not Prevent the Students from Protecting Themselves

The fact that "the specific threat at issue in this case" was "a violent bully subject to two restraining orders" does not necessarily give rise to a special relationship. The restraining orders to which the dissent refers were addressed to Anderson, not the Defendants, and the orders themselves do not impose any affirmative duties on the Defendants. Indeed, we very much doubt that any Defendant was a party to the proceedings that resulted in the orders, and no such involvement has been alleged. Although the Defendants, and other third parties, are prohibited from making contact with the Morrow children *on Anderson's behalf,* the no-contact orders cannot reasonably be interpreted as imposing any obligation on the Defendants to ensure Anderson's compliance with the orders or to otherwise enforce them.

Moreover, whether our dissenting colleagues are referencing the school's "No Tolerance Policy," or the policy that allegedly required Anderson's expulsion from school, in arguing that the Defendants "enforced school policies that prevented the Morrows from being fully able to protect themselves," neither the mere existence of such common disciplinary policies, nor the school's exercise of discretion in enforcing them, altered the relationship between the school and its students to the extent required to create a constitutional duty under the Supreme Court's precedent. . . .

The Constitution Does Not Have an Answer for Every Problem in Society

We reiterate that we both appreciate the Morrows' concerns and that we are sympathetic to their plight. Parents in their position should be able to send their children off to school with some level of comfort that those children will be safe from bullies such as Anderson and her confederate. Indeed, the increasing prevalence of the kind of bullying alleged here has generated considerable discussion and legislative action. Nonetheless, "the Constitution does not provide judicial remedies for every social . . . ill." *Lindsey v. Normet* (1972). Given the limitations of *DeShaney,* and the language in *Vernonia,* it is now clear that the redress the Morrows seek must come from a source other than the United States Constitution.

Our dissenting colleagues take us to task for expressing concern for the Morrows' plight without providing a remedy and suggest that the very fact that we are troubled by the result counsels in favor of a constitutional remedy. . . .

However, "the due process clause is not a surrogate for local tort law or state statutory and administrative remedies." *Hasenfus v. LaJeunesse* (1st Cir. 1999). Nor is "[s]ubstantive due process . . . a license for judges to supersede the decisions of local officials and elected legislators on such matters." *Id.*

"The desires to nurture and protect have become major components in the recent anti-bullying efforts."

Overattentive Parents May Be Contributing to the Bullying Problem

Joseph Simplicio

In the following viewpoint, Joseph Simplicio, an education profes- sor, argues that recent parenting trends, defined by intense involve- ment of parents in all phases of their children's lives, have led to an increase in the bullying problem. The author asserts that parents' tendency to overprotect their children, shield them from competi- tion and losing, and support them financially well into early adult- hood has created a situation in which children never develop inde- pendence or learn to take care of themselves. These tendencies have also led to the implementation of anti-bullying policies in schools that in the author's view continue this cycle of dependence and gives students an excuse to take physical action against their tor- menters. Simplicio maintains that the best approach to addressing bullying is to instill in children the ability to handle their problems

Joseph Simplicio, "Suck It Up, Walk It Off, Be a Man: A Controversial Look at Bullying in Today's Schools," *Education*, vol. 133, Spring 2013. Copyright © 2013 by Education. All rights reserved. Reproduced by permission.

on their own. Joseph Simplicio holds a PhD in education from New York University and has served as an administrator at all levels in higher education.

The latest issue to permeate the educational collective mind is that of bullying. According to some educators the problem of bullying within our nation's schools has grown to epidemic proportions.

These individuals point to the fact that connections have even been made between this problem and more serious ones, such as school shootings. A recent [2002] Department of Education study on school violence indicted that bullying was a key factor in some of the recent school shootings. "Almost three-quarters of the attackers felt persecuted, bullied, threatened, attacked, or injured by others prior to the incident."

Bullying Has a Range of Definitions

Bullying has been defined as treating others ". . . abusively by means of force or coercion" (Merriam-Webster, 2012), and ". . . in an overbearing or intimidating manner" (The Free Dictionary, 2012). A bully then is a ". . . person who is habitually cruel or overbearing, especially to smaller or weaker people" (The Free Dictionary, 2012).

According to Kate Anton at the YMCA Crisis Center in Enid, Oklahoma, bullying can take several forms. It can be coercion; threats; intimidation; abuse; social isolation; humiliation, as well as other less direct forms. Bullying is usually habitual and often causes a cycle of continual fear amongst its victims.

Bullying can be physical, verbal, and even emotional. Physical bullying, which is defined as "any physical contact that would hurt or injure a person . . . accounts for approximately 30.5% of all bullying" (Library Think Quest, 2012).

Verbal bullying, including name calling and making offensive remarks, accounts for 46.5% of all bullying in schools (Library Think Quest, 2012).

Indirect bullying such as spreading rumors occurs in 18.5% of all bullying incidents (Library Think Quest, 2012).

Bullying can even occur through the Internet. Cyberbullying relies on sending messages or pictures through computers, cell phones, or by way of social media. Statistically it is included in the category of "other types" of bullying and occurs in about 4% of all bullying cases.

As might be expected females are more likely to use verbal and social methods while their male counterparts rely on the use of physical violence more often.

In all cases bullying is a result of an imbalance of power. As a result, it is clear that bullying is an important issue that is facing today's schools throughout the nation. The author understands the gravity of the situation and in no way wishes to minimize the problem or condone bullying in any form.

New Generations Must Be Understood to Understand Bullying Today

While this is true it is also important to discuss the issue from an academic and scholarly perspective and to explore the "I wonder ifs" of the problem. Since the definition of bullying is so inclusive, to do so, we must first ask just how bad is it in actuality within our schools?

The Melissa Institute's Scientific Board found that the problem of bullying ". . . is very serious for only 10%" of the student population and only . . . 20% will require some kind of intervention and support (2012). These statistics hardly support the claim that this problem is of epic proportions.

To truly understand bullying we must also understand today's students. Today's students are a melding of two identifiable generations. First there are those of Generation Z. This generation, also known as Generation I because of its heavy exposure and involvement with the Internet, was ". . . born between the years 1994–2004" (I Media Connection, 2012).

The second group of students has been identified as Generation AO. These children were born in the early 2000s. The term AO, which signifies "Always On," meaning always con-

US first lady Michelle Obama exercises with children from Orr Elementary School in Washington, DC, in 2013 as part of her Let's Move! program. Some believe the current generation of children is too dependent on technology while not getting enough physical activity and human interaction. © Win McNamee/Getty Images.

nected to some form of Internet access, was first coined by Janna Quitney Anderson of Elon University. "The children of Gen AO are being born into lives in which they have instant access nearly everywhere to nearly the entirety of human knowledge" (Mind of the Geek, 2012).

These young individuals are unlike any other generation that this nation has fostered. Reflecting the age of technology in which they were born and raised they have been nurtured with a completely different set of parenting strategies that have marked them as individualistically unique within American history.

A better understanding of these children and their role in American society will shed new light on the bullying dilemma.

Parents Have Become Much More Active in Their Children's Lives

What makes these generations of children so unique is the manner in which they were raised. Their parents adopted child rearing strategies that were well meaning and yet questionable in many ways.

These parents have come to be known by several new names. They are the "helicopter parents" because of the way they constantly hover around their children in attempts to protect and guide them. They help their children do everything from homework to organizing play dates to finding a job.

The more aggressive helicopter parents have been labeled "lawnmower parents" because of their willingness to "mow down" anyone who gets in the way of their children's success. Even more protective are the "On-Star parents" who provide their children with concierge service upon request.

The once docile parents who would humbly sit and listen to a classroom teacher regarding their child's poor academic performance or misbehavior in class have now been be replaced by fire breathing, litigating, and career threatening parents.

This trend does not appear to be changing. A recent *Times Magazine* article explored the latest parenting phenomenon known as Attachment Parenting. Its leading proponent, Dr. Bill Sears, advocates breast feeding on demand and into toddlerhood, not allowing any child to cry without being comforted immediately, and co-sleeping with young children. This theory in essence creates a constant physical bond between parents and children, with emphasis on the word "constant."

Parents are even warned [in this article] that "excessive crying over prolonged periods can damage an infant's brain." This claim has been vehemently disputed within the scientific community and yet, many parents still believe that Dr. Sears is correct and thus act accordingly.

As a result of this shift in parenting techniques parents now serve as pseudo friends. They do not want their children to dislike them or to be angry with them. These efforts, although meant with the best of intentions, have created role confusion between parents and their children.

Children Today Lack Preparation for the Real World

Today's children have been protected and nurtured to the point that they have not been allowed to fail on any level. Competition has been replaced with everyone receiving a trophy and sporting events where no one keeps score for fear that someone will lose and feelings will be hurt. Effort alone now substitutes for success. No winners and no losers though mean that children receive no tangible life experience as they grow to maturity. Eventually, these young adults are exposed to a real world filled with competition where individuals win and lose every day in business, relationships, and all of life's situations. Having never experienced real failure many are unable to cope with this reality.

Children as a result have also come to rely on their parents in ways no other generation has in the past. This is a primary reason why so many young adults have deferred leaving home. It is just too comfortable to stay with their parents taking care of everything from room and board, to automobiles, to medical insurance, to cell phones, to maid service, and more.

This phenomenon has spilled over into the real world as parents continue to guard their children even into adulthood. To meet the demands of meddling parents for example, some businesses have been forced to introduce a "parents' package" which is given to new young employees. This package highlights policies and concerns that parents may have concerning their child's new career. This was a direct business response to parental interference with the daily operation of business that included threatening telephone calls to supervisors and continual demands by parents on behalf of their children for better benefits or compensation. It appears that the umbilical cord will never be severed for many parents.

Children Interact with Technology, Not Other Humans

These are also the generations of children that have come to age in a technological world where entertainment often means interacting with computers and video games instead of backyard baseball or football.

It is an alarming and somewhat sad reality that the larger community has been forced to mount organized efforts to cajole its children to put down the video controllers and go outside to play.

There are public, private, business, and government initiatives on the local, state, national and even international levels designed to get children out of the house and involved in some form of physical activity.

The National Football League's "Play 60" for example is the league's "campaign to encourage kids to be active for 60 minutes a day . . ." (Play 60, 2012).

The "Let's Move" Program developed by First Lady Michelle Obama is a campaign that claims "Physical activity is an essential component of a healthy lifestyle . . ." (Let's Move, 2012).

Even international efforts, such as the Canadian Goodlife Kids Foundation Grant Project, believe that "being active is not only good for the body and mind but also a lot of fun" (2012).

All these efforts have one simple goal and that is to get children outside and involved in physical activities because it is "good for them."

Duh! Really? Talk about a "no brainer." Do our children actually have to be taught this lesson?

Concern About Bullying Has Led to Changes in School Policy

The desires to nurture and protect have become major components in the recent anti-bullying efforts.

The topic of bullying in schools has become the flavor of the month in education. It has been explored through documentaries such as the "Bully Project;" through writings and poems; in the sharing of stories anonymously; through local school initiatives, and through state, national, and international projects.

It has caused changes in school curricula, and new types of lesson plans, teaching strategies, and methodologies have been developed to deal with the issue. Guides have been created for teachers, parents, and students alike telling them how to deal with bullies. Even social media, including Facebook and Twitter, have been drafted into the anti-bullying movement.

The vast majority of these strategies tell children who feel threatened to "go tell someone." Students are encouraged to "tell on" their fellow classmates who they believe to be bullies. Feelings substitute for actions and children who do not feel safe can simply report this to someone in authority and that adult will take the appropriate action.

In light of all these efforts schools have developed "zero tolerance" policies that lead to immediate suspension for anyone involved in an altercation. Under many of these policies students who are attacked are not even allowed to defend themselves without getting into trouble themselves.

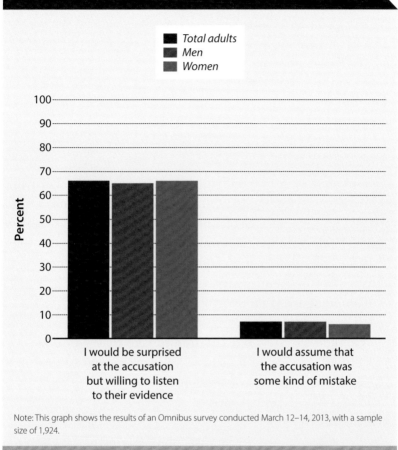

PARENTS' REACTIONS TO ACCUSATIONS THEIR CHILDREN WERE BULLYING

- Total adults
- Men
- Women

Percent

I would be surprised at the accusation but willing to listen to their evidence

I would assume that the accusation was some kind of mistake

Note: This graph shows the results of an Omnibus survey conducted March 12–14, 2013, with a sample size of 1,924.

Taken from: Ray Martin, "Children and Bullying—How Do Their Parents React?," YouGov, March 22, 2013.

The Response to Bullying Raises Many Questions

What is interesting about the concept of bullying is the fact that very often it is difficult to prove that someone was not bullied. In many cases there is simply no way an individual can disprove the charge of bullying.

All of this raises some very interesting questions.

First, has bullying become an excuse for individuals taking actions against each other? In a recent stabbing at a school bus stop in Florida for example, the attacker accused the person he stabbed of having bullied him, even though the stabbing victim had no weapon. The result was that to date no one has been charged with any crime.

Is simply crying "wolf" or in this case "bully" justifiable cause for taking action, even violent action, against another human being?

If bullying cannot be disproved, then is everyone who hurts someone else's feeling fair game?

More importantly, if bullying is indeed a serious and growing problem, have we extended our parental and communal shields around these generations of children to the point where they are incapable of handling this problem themselves?

Is this yet another indication of parents fighting their children's battles for them again?

If so, what does that teach them?

When is enough, enough?

When do we allow our children to take charge of their own lives, even if that means they have to learn through failure?

Children Must Learn to Be Independent

These are difficult questions indeed, but if we truly want to teach our children to be successful we must first teach them to be independent individuals who are willing to take risks. Just like the rest of us, one day they will have to learn to work out their problems with others. Just like the rest of us, one day they will have to learn how to deal with adversity on their own. Just like the rest of us, one day they will have to learn how to take responsibility and learn to be accountable for their own actions.

Finally, just like the rest of us, one day they are going to have to learn to grow up.

Maybe that one day should be today.

> "Children torment other children. At
> what point in history has this not been
> the case?"

A Former Lawyer Compares the Overreaction He Sees to Bullying Today with the Nonresponse He Experienced as a Youth

Personal Narrative

Elie Mystal

Elie Mystal, a man who experienced physical and emotional bully-ing as a youth, tells how the response to bullying differed when he was young and how the reaction of his parents, school, and society helped him to become a successful adult. Mystal details occasions when he was beat up as a youth, suffered humiliation as a result of the bullying, and was even blamed by his parents for getting into a situation where he was bullied. The author asserts that his parents' response taught him how to handle bullying, a lesson that served him not only as a child but throughout his adult life when he experienced embarrassment and disappointment. Mystal urges parents to recognize that bullying is a part of growing up and that it teaches kids essential lessons about life. Elie Mystal holds a JD from Harvard Law School, but quit a career as a lawyer to write for online and print publications such as Above the Law, *the* New York Daily News, *and the* New York Times *and to appear as a commentator on cable television news channels.*

They had to set the *Karate Kid* remake in China. If they had set it in modern-day America, Daniel-san would have been mercilessly bullied by the kids from Cobra Kai, he would have killed himself, and the rest of the movie would have been a courtroom drama where Daniel's parents sought to bring the evil sensei to justice in the form of a multi-million dollar civil suit.

You see, American children apparently have become so fragile, and Americans parents so litigious, that schoolyard bullying is as likely to be settled in a court of law as it is behind a dumpster out back where boys used to handle their disagreements. I used to tell my mother that nobody ever died from embarrassment, but apparently I was wrong. The *ABA Journal* reports that there's been a veritable outbreak of children committing suicide in Ohio because they were hounded by mean kids. And that story doesn't even take into account the Tyler Clementi situation [Clementi, a Rutgers University student, committed suicide after his roommate posted a video of him kissing another man].

And when kids kill themselves, parents are increasingly turning to the courts to stand up to the bullies in a way that used to be accomplished via a flush crane-kick to the face.

Bullying Is Unavoidable

It needs to stop. No, not the bullying—which is *unavoidable* when more than one male competes for whatever status/prestige/sex is on offer—but the tragic overreactions to the bullying, and the accompanying rush to the courthouse steps.

I say this not as an alpha-male with a cavalier attitude towards the feelings of others. I say this as a former omega-male who got the crap beat out of me like I stole something from the age of 7 through the point I realized that no girl would ever mate with a guy who couldn't basically stand up for himself. . . .

I wasn't always this big or this strong. As a kid, I was a polite, articulate little boy who did well in school. Or "Oreo fa**ot," as my friends liked to call me. I've shared some of my childhood scrapes before—and I still hate Halloween.

My best story (it's funny now, I think) involves me trying to walk a girl home from school when I was 12. She was walking, I was walking and rolling my bike, and then the bullies spotted us. As they approached, she said, "It's okay, you can run." And I did—I hopped on my bike and booked out of there. They were on foot, so I easily put some distance between us. I looked back and flipped the head bully (we'll call him "Lewis" because his name is Lewis and he's in jail now so he can't read this) the finger. But that took my eyes off the road—and the tree branch in front of me. Bad times. I tumbled, they caught up, and then five kids proceeded to twist my flimsy bike around me. They got both wheels around me, and I had to waddle the rest of the way home. I was a latchkey kid, and I couldn't reach my keys since my arms were effectively pinned to my body and I couldn't reach my pockets. I had to sit on my stoop for hours (which felt like days), until my parents came home to let me inside (and take me to the bike shop to free me).

Suicide to Escape Bullying Was Not an Option

What did I learn from all this? Well, nothing. Not really. Don't take your eyes off the road? Yeah, already pretty much aware of that one buddy, didn't need to be beaten and humiliated for the lesson to stick. People who used to get beat up in school always try to find some character-building value from their experience. But usually, it's total BS. Sure, much of my what I call "wit" was forged in the crucible of trying to come up with something biting to say because I couldn't defend myself. But I'm confident I could have learned an appropriate amount of snark without getting bikes wrapped around me.

The only thing I learned from getting beat up all the time that I couldn't have learned had I not constantly gotten my ass kicked was that it sucks to get beat up all the time. And once I grew into my body a little bit more, the beatings stopped. Or was it that my parents finally, mercifully moved me to a private school, so that instead of facing my demons I could just graduate to a better socioeconomic class where it would be harder for them to find me?

The point is, I'm happy to say, I never killed myself. Beaten and humiliated? Yes. Taking my own life? No. Even at the time, killing myself felt like an overreaction. I didn't want to kill myself; I wanted to kill *them*. And boy, did I have plans for making that happen. Hell . . . I *still have a plan* for what happens when Lewis gets out of jail. Because that's what men do. They defend themselves, or they make plans for defending themselves sometime in the future.

Parents Should Teach Their Kids How to Deal with Being Bullied

I learned that from my parents, who (to their credit) did not overreact. Did they ever take one of my tormentors to court? Hell no. They never even brought up my bullying to any of my tormentors' parents. I'll never forget the Christmas party my parents threw where Lewis showed up to my house. Later, when he was beating me in the head with a Nintendo cartridge, his parents yelled at him . . . and my parents yelled at me, for "starting some s**t with a bigger kid when you can't defend yourself."

What my parents knew, and what I've learned over the years, is that in life there will always be bullies—and there will always be people who are being bullied. And you are not going to be very successful in life if you don't know how to handle both roles because you'll have to play one or the other from time to time. It's the job of parents to teach their kids how to handle being bullied, being embarrassed, and being humiliated. It happens to all of us,

SUICIDE RATE BY AGE, 2000–2010

14 and under
15 to 24
25 to 44
45 to 64
65 to 84
85 and over

Age-Adjusted Rate

20%

15%

10%

5%

2000 2001 2002 2003 2004 2005 2006 2007 2008 2009 2010
Year

Note: The suicide rate as calculated by the Centers for Disease Control and Prevention measures the number of suicides per one hundred thousand people.

Taken from: American Foundation for Suicide Prevention, Facts and Figures, Centers for Disease Control and Prevention, 2010.

and if it hasn't happened to you yet, just wait. You think it's not humiliating to go to law school and then get shut out from the job market? You think it's not embarrassing to get way too drunk at a firm event and end up on Above the Law? These things happen to people everyday. What are you going to do when it happens to you—run to court?

And there are a lot of people out there who say "yes, that's exactly what I'll do, I'll run to court the minute anything bad happens to me." That's your right, but it doesn't make it right. If nothing else, it sets a terrible example for your children. It tells them that at the slightest provocation you'll run to the system to help you out of trouble. So what will they do if they don't feel the system can help them? Have you given them the sense that they can and should be able to handle certain things on their own?

Bullies Don't Try to Make Kids Kill Themselves

If we did charge every bully with the crime of being a bully, how far are we willing to take this thing? Are we going to charge every little girl who says "that backpack is sooo last year"? Are we going to charge every boss who gives overly strong handshakes and talks loudly around weak men? I don't like slippery slope arguments, but people get bullied in one form or another everyday. We can't charge all of them, so why should we charge just the ones who happen to have a victim who takes the *extraordinary* step of ending his or her own life? Look at the scope of bullying captured in the Ohio cases:

> Two other youths at the high school committed suicide and a third died after taking an overdose of antidepressants. One was bullied for being gay, another for having a learning disability, and a third for being a boy who liked to wear pink.

Yes, parents: boys are going to make fun of the effeminate kid. They're also going to make fun of the slow kid. And I've been making fun of the professional football players who have been wearing pink all month—even though they're only wearing it to support breast cancer awareness.

In other news, boys will also torment the fat kid, the thin kid, the kid with a bad haircut, the kid with the lisp, the kid who gets all the math problems right, the kid who gets all the math problems wrong, the kid with the ugly mom, hot mom, or two moms. *Children torment other children.* At what point in history has this not been the case?

Not every torment is not a crime, and not every bully is a criminal. You could say that I was a victim of bullying; you could say that I was a victim of *repeated physical assaults.* Both are true. But you can't say that the bullies tried to make me kill myself.

We're talking about tormentors, not torturers.

> *"Public schools have a 'compelling interest' in regulating speech that interferes with or disrupts the work and discipline of the school, including discipline for student harassment and bullying."*

Schools Can Punish Students for Cyberbullying That Occurs Outside School

US Circuit Court Ruling

Paul V. Niemeyer

Kara Kowalski, a senior at West Virginia's Musselman High School in Berkeley County, began a MySpace site in December 2005 called S.A.S.H. The acronym was said to mean both Students Against Sluts Herpes and Students Against Shay's Herpes, referring to a particular student, Shay N., who was the topic of most of the derogatory posts on the page. After the school was informed about the site by Shay's parents, Kowalski received a five-day out-of-school suspension and ninety-day social suspension, preventing her from participating in social events and the cheerleading squad, for her violation of the school's Harassment, Bullying, and Intimidation Policy. Kowalski then sued the school for violating her free speech and due process rights. In the following viewpoint, US Circuit Court judge

Paul V. Niemeyer, *Kowalski v. Berkeley County Schools*, US Circuit Court, July 27, 2011.

Paul V. Niemeyer rules to uphold the school's punishment, finding that it did not violate the teen's First or Fourteenth Amendment rights. Niemeyer maintains that schools have the right to punish individuals whose conduct, including speech, creates a school environment disruptive to learning. While he concedes that the punished speech did occur outside of school, he asserts that because the speech was directed at a fellow student and was created with the intention of reaching the school and students, school officials had an interest in curtailing the speech and its effect on campus. Paul V. Niemeyer was appointed to the US Court of Appeals for the Fourth Circuit in 1990.

When Kara Kowalski was a senior at Musselman High School in Berkeley County, West Virginia, school administrators suspended her from school for five days for creating and posting to a MySpace.com webpage called "S.A.S.H.," which Kowalski claims stood for "Students Against Sluts Herpes" and which was largely dedicated to ridiculing a fellow student. Kowalski commenced this action, under 42 U.S.C. § 1983, against the Berkeley County School District and five of its officers, contending that in disciplining her, the defendants violated her free speech and due process rights under the First and Fourteenth Amendments. She alleges, among other things, that the School District was not justified in regulating her speech because it did not occur during a "school-related activity," but rather was "private out-of-school speech."

The district court entered summary judgment in favor of the defendants, concluding that they were authorized to punish Kowalski because her webpage was "created for the purpose of inviting others to indulge in disruptive and hateful conduct," which caused an "in-school disruption."

Reviewing the summary judgment record *de novo* [anew], we conclude that in the circumstances of this case, the School District's imposition of sanctions was permissible. Kowalski used the Internet to orchestrate a targeted attack on a classmate, and did so in a manner that was sufficiently connected to the school environment as to implicate the School District's recognized authority to discipline speech which "materially and substantially interfere[es] with the requirements of appropriate discipline in the operation of the school and collid[es] with the rights of others." *Tinker v. Des Moines Indep. Community Sch. Dist.* (1969) (internal quotation marks omitted). Accordingly, we affirm. . . .

Schools Can Limit Students' First Amendment Rights at School

Kowalski contends first that the school administrators violated her free speech rights under the First Amendment by punishing her for speech that occurred outside the school. She argues that because this case involved "off-campus, non-school related speech," school administrators had no power to discipline her. As she asserts, "The [Supreme] Court has been consistently careful to limit intrusions on students' rights to conduct taking place on school property, at school functions, or while engaged in school-sponsored or school-sanctioned activity." She maintains that "no Supreme Court case addressing student speech has held that a school may punish students for speech away from school—indeed every Supreme Court case addressing student speech has taken pains to emphasize that, were the speech in question to occur away from school, it would be protected."

The Berkeley County School District and its administrators contend that school officials "may regulate off-campus behavior insofar as the off-campus behavior creates a foreseeable risk of reaching school property and causing a substantial disruption to the work and discipline of the school," citing *Doninger v. Niehoff* (2d Cir. 2008). Relying on *Doninger*, the defendants note that Kowalski created a webpage that singled out Shay N. for harassment, bullying and intimidation; that it was foreseeable that the off-campus conduct would reach the school; and that it was foreseeable that the off-campus conduct would "create a substantial disruption in the school."

The question thus presented is whether Kowalski's activity fell within the outer boundaries of the high school's legitimate interest in maintaining order in the school and protecting the well-being and educational rights of its students.

The First Amendment prohibits Congress and, through the Fourteenth Amendment, the States from "abridging the freedom of speech." It is a "bedrock principle" of the First Amendment that "the government may not prohibit the expression of an idea simply because society finds the idea itself offensive or disagreeable." *Texas v. Johnson* (1989).

While students retain significant First Amendment rights in the school context, their rights are not coextensive with those of adults. Because of the "special characteristics of the school environment," [*Tinker v. Des Moines Indep. Community Sch. Dist.* (1969)] school administrators have some latitude in regulating student speech to further educational objectives. Thus in *Tinker*, the Court held that student speech, consisting of wearing armbands in political protest against the Vietnam War, was protected because it did not "'materially and substantially interfer[e] with the requirements of appropriate discipline in the operation of the school' [or] collid[e] with the rights of others," and thus did not "materially disrupt[ ] classwork or involve[ ] substantial disorder or invasion of the rights of others." Student speech also may be regulated if it is otherwise "vulgar and lewd." *Bethel Sch. Dist. No. 403 v. Fraser* (1986). Finally, the Supreme Court has held that school administrators are free to regulate and punish student speech that encourages the use of illegal drugs. *Morse v. Frederick* (2007).

Speech That Does Not Disrupt School Is Protected

Although the Supreme Court has not dealt specifically with a factual circumstance where student speech targeted classmates for verbal abuse, in *Tinker* it recognized the need for regulation of speech that interfered with the school's work and discipline,

In Kowalski v. Berkeley County Schools (2011), the US Court of Appeals for the Fourth Circuit ruled that schools can punish students for cyberbullying outside of school if it creates an environment disruptive to learning. © Istockphoto.com/ClarkandCompany.

describing that interference as speech that "disrupts classwork," creates "substantial disorder," or "collid[es] with" or "inva[des]" "the rights of others."

In *Tinker*, the Court pointed out at length how wearing black armbands in protest against the Vietnam War was passive and did not create "disorder or disturbance" and therefore did not interfere with the school's work or collide with other students' rights "to be secure and to be let alone." Of course, a mere desire to avoid "discomfort and unpleasantness" was an insufficient basis to regulate the speech; there had to be disruption in the sense that the speech "would materially and substantially interfere with the requirements of appropriate discipline in the operation of the school." [*Tinker* (1969).] The Court amplified the nature of the disruption it had in mind when it stated:

> [C]onduct by [a] student, in class or out of it, which for any reason—whether it stems from time, place, or type of behavior —materially disrupts classwork or involves substantial disorder or invasion of the rights of others is, of course, not immunized by the constitutional guarantee of freedom of speech.

The *Tinker* Court referred to this amplified statement of its test later in its opinion in shorthand when it concluded that the regulation of armbands "would violate the constitutional rights of students, at least if it could not be justified by a showing that the students' activities would materially and substantially disrupt *the work and discipline of the school.*" *Id.* (emphasis added). Because, in *Tinker*, the students' wearing of the armbands "neither interrupted school activities nor sought to intrude in the school affairs or the lives of others," there was "no interference with work and no disorder" to justify regulation of the speech.

Thus, the language of *Tinker* supports the conclusion that public schools have a "compelling interest" in regulating speech that interferes with or disrupts the work and discipline of the school, including discipline for student harassment and bullying.

School Administrations Must Act to Maintain a Safe School Environment

According to a federal government initiative, student-on-student bullying is a "major concern" in schools across the country and can cause victims to become depressed and anxious, to be afraid to go to school, and to have thoughts of suicide. Just as schools have a responsibility to provide a safe environment for students free from messages advocating illegal drug use, schools have a duty to protect their students from harassment and bullying in the school environment. Far from being a situation where school authorities "suppress speech on political and social issues based on disagreement with the viewpoint expressed," *Morse*, school administrators must be able to prevent and punish harassment and bullying in order to provide a safe school environment conducive to learning.

We are confident that Kowalski's speech caused the interference and disruption described in *Tinker* as being immune from First Amendment protection. The "S.A.S.H." webpage functioned as a platform for Kowalski and her friends to direct verbal attacks towards classmate Shay N. The webpage contained comments accusing Shay N. of having herpes and being a "slut," as well as photographs reinforcing those defamatory accusations by depicting a sign across her pelvic area, which stated, "Warning: Enter at your own risk" and labeling her portrait as that of a "whore." One student's posting dismissed any concern for Shay N.'s reaction with a comment that said, "screw her." This is not the conduct and speech that our educational system is required to tolerate, as schools attempt to educate students about "habits and manners of civility" or the "fundamental values necessary to the maintenance of a democratic political system." *Fraser*.

While Kowalski does not seriously dispute the harassing character of the speech on the "S.A.S.H." webpage, she argues mainly that her conduct took place at home after school and that the forum she created was therefore subject to the full protection of the First Amendment. This argument, however, raises the metaphysical question of where her speech occurred when she used the Internet as the medium. Kowalski indeed pushed her computer's keys in her home, but she knew that the electronic response would be, as it in fact was, published beyond her home and could reasonably be expected to reach the school or impact the school environment. She also knew that the dialogue would and did take place among Musselman High School students whom she invited to join the "S.A.S.H." group and that the fall-out from her conduct and the speech within the group would be felt in the school itself. Indeed, the group's name was "*Students Against Sluts Herpes*" and a vast majority of its members were Musselman students. As one commentator on the webpage observed, "wait til [Shay N.] sees the page lol." Moreover, as Kowalski could anticipate, Shay N. and her parents took the attack as having been made in the school context, as they went to the high school to lodge their complaint.

There is surely a limit to the scope of a high school's interest in the order, safety, and well-being of its students when the speech at issue originates outside the schoolhouse gate. But we need not fully define that limit here, as we are satisfied that the nexus of Kowalski's speech to Musselman High School's pedagogical interests was sufficiently strong to justify the action taken by school officials in carrying out their role as the trustees of the student body's well-being.

Speech Conducted off School Grounds Can Be Punished by the School

Of course, had Kowalski created the "S.A.S.H." group during school hours, using a school-provided computer and Internet connection, this case would be more clear-cut, as the question of where speech that was transmitted by the Internet "occurred" would not come into play. To be sure, a court could determine that speech originating outside of the schoolhouse gate but directed at persons in school and received by and acted on by them was in fact in-school speech. In that case, because it was determined to be in-school speech, its regulation would be permissible not only under *Tinker* but also, as vulgar and lewd in-school speech, under *Fraser*. We need not resolve, however, whether this was in-school speech and therefore whether *Fraser* could apply because the School District was authorized by *Tinker* to discipline Kowalski, regardless of where her speech originated, because the speech was materially and substantially disruptive in that it "interfer[ed] . . . with the schools' work [and] colli[ded] with the rights of other students to be secure and to be let alone." *See Tinker.*

Given the targeted, defamatory nature of Kowalski's speech, aimed at a fellow classmate, it created "actual or nascent" substantial disorder and disruption in the school. First, the creation of the "S.A.S.H." group forced Shay N. to miss school in order to avoid further abuse. Moreover, had the school not intervened, the potential for continuing and more serious harassment of Shay N. as well as other students was real. Experience suggests that unpunished misbehavior can have a snowballing effect, in some cases resulting in "copycat" efforts by other students or in retaliation for the initial harassment.

Other courts have similarly concluded that school administrators' authority to regulate student speech extends, in the appropriate circumstances, to speech that does not originate at the school itself, so long as the speech eventually makes its way to the school in a meaningful way. For example, in *Boucher v. School Board of School District of Greenfield* (7th Cir. 1998), the Seventh Circuit held that a student was not entitled to a preliminary injunction prohibiting his punishment when the student wrote articles for an independent newspaper that was distributed at school. And again in *Doninger*, the Second Circuit concluded, after a student applied for a preliminary injunction in a factual circumstance not unlike the one at hand, that a school could discipline a student for an out-of-school blog post that included vulgar language and misleading information about school administrators, as long as it was reasonably foreseeable that the post would reach the school and create a substantial disruption there. The court explained, "a student may be disciplined for expressive conduct, even conduct occurring off school grounds, when this conduct 'would foreseeably create a risk of substantial disruption within the school environment,' at least when it was

Punishment for Cyberbullying Does Not Infringe on Students' Free Speech

Schools have a greater need for regulating students' speech with the recent cyberbullying outbreak. With the prevalent use of mobile devices and social media, cyberbullying has become a daily concern for school administrators. According to recent statistics, approximately one million students were subjected to some form of cyberbullying on Facebook alone in the year 2011. Furthermore, about 20% of students claim they have been bullied through the Internet. Some cyberbullying is considered more of a nuisance than a threat, but if a student bullies another student or teacher and that communication can be characterized as a threat, the school should be able to properly discipline that student without violating his or her free speech rights. . . . Schools should not have to tolerate threatening speech made by their students towards other students or school employees, and the true threat doctrine could provide one alternative to handle this type of speech in the school context.

Jessica K. Boyd, "Moving the Bully from the Schoolyard to Cyberspace: How Much Protection Is Off-Campus Speech Awarded Under the First Amendment?," Alabama Law Review, *2013.*

similarly foreseeable that the off-campus expression might also reach campus."

Thus, even though Kowalski was not physically at the school when she operated her computer to create the webpage and form the "S.A.S.H." MySpace group and to post comments there, other circuits have applied *Tinker* to such circumstances. To be sure, it was foreseeable in this case that Kowalski's conduct would reach the school via computers, smartphones, and other electronic devices, given that most of the "S.A.S.H." group's members and the target of the group's harassment were Musselman High School students. Indeed, the "S.A.S.H." webpage did make its way into the school and was accessed first by Musselman student Ray Parsons at 3:40 p.m., from a school computer during an after hours class. Furthermore, as we have noted, it created a reasonably foreseeable substantial disruption there.

At bottom, we conclude that the school was authorized to discipline Kowalski because her speech interfered with the work and discipline of the school. . . .

Schools Maintain the Right to Punish Behavior That Prevents Education

Kowalski's role in the "S.A.S.H." webpage, which was used to ridicule and demean a fellow student, was particularly mean-spirited and hateful. The webpage called on classmates, in a pack, to target Shay N., knowing that it would be hurtful and damaging to her ability to sit with other students in class at Musselman High School and have a suitable learning experience. While each student in the "S.A.S.H." group might later attempt to minimize his or her role, at bottom, the conduct was indisputably harassing and bullying, in violation of Musselman High School's regulations prohibiting such conduct.

Kowalski asserts that the protections of free speech and due process somehow insulate her activities from school discipline because her activity was not sufficiently school-related to be subject to school discipline. Yet, every aspect of the webpage's design and implementation was school-related. Kowalski designed the website for "students," perhaps even against Shay N.; she sent it to students inviting them to join; and those who joined were mostly students, with Kowalski encouraging the commentary. The victim understood the attack as school-related, filing her complaint with school authorities. Ray Parsons, who provided the vulgar and lewd—indeed, defamatory—photographs understood that the object of the attack was Shay N., and he participated from a school computer during class, to the cheering of Kowalski and her fellow classmates, whom she invited to the affair.

Rather than respond constructively to the school's efforts to bring order and provide a lesson following the incident, Kowalski has rejected those efforts and sued school authorities for damages and other relief. Regretfully, she yet fails to see that such harassment and bullying is inappropriate and hurtful and that it must be taken seriously by school administrators in order to preserve an appropriate pedagogical environment. Indeed, school administrators *are* becoming increasingly alarmed by the phenomenon, and the events in this case are but one example of such bullying and school administrators' efforts to contain it. Suffice it to hold here that, where such speech has a sufficient nexus with the school, the Constitution is not written to hinder school administrators' good faith efforts to address the problem.

11

> "The substantial disruption test will continue to burden school officials who have the responsibility of evaluating the level of disruption occurring [to a student's education]."

The Supreme Court Should Rule on Cyberbullying

Carolyn Stone

In the following viewpoint, Carolyn Stone, a professor at the University of North Florida and the ethics chair of the American School Counselor Association, argues that cyberbulling is disruptive to students' education and should not be protected free speech, and thus, clear guidelines should be established for how schools should address the issue in the form of a US Supreme Court ruling. Stone describes the variety of rulings in US Circuit Court cases regarding students' right to free speech even when it is disruptive to other students' education and maintains that any response by the school is a risk because no standard has been established regarding what disciplinary action should be taken. She contends that the best way to determine these standards would be through a Supreme Court ruling on the issue and urges the court to address this topic promptly.

Carolyn Stone, "Cyber Bullying: Disruptive Conduct or Free Speech," *ASCA School Counselor*, May 1, 2013. Copyright © 2013 by ASCA School Counselor. All rights reserved. Reproduced by permission.

*O*ne of your counselees, Rachel, comes to you distraught that she was being called a "slut with herpes" by her classmate Sarah online. Sarah asked others to join her online in humiliating Rachel. You assure Rachel that something will be done to help her. You take her case to the principal, who expresses concern for Rachel and disciplines Sarah with in-school suspension. Rachel and her parents are tremendously relieved and thank you and the principal.

OR

You take this case to the principal, who expresses concern for Rachel but is quick to tell you her hands are tied as far as being able to discipline Sarah. The principal explains that Sarah has a right to off-campus free speech unless her cyber-speech causes a substantial disruption to the educational environment or such a disruption can be predicted. The principal says all she can do at this point is bring Sarah and her parents in and request they cooperate and remove the offending material. You are distressed to think there is no recourse for this student other than hoping the bully will behave.

Legally, which of the above actions is the correct response?

The Courts Do Not Give Educators Clear Guidelines When It Comes to Cyberbullying

Currently the courts don't agree on this issue, and administrators do not have a clear-cut standard they can use to regulate and punish online speech. Principals take a risk regardless of which way they choose to go. However, in January 2012, relief was on the way when three student cyber-speech cases made it to the U.S. Supreme Court: *Kowalski v. Berkeley County School District* in West Virginia, *J.S. v. Blue Mountain School District* and *Layshock v. Hermitage School District*.

In the Kowalski case, Kara Kowalski was disciplined for beginning a MySpace page that successfully invited others to make offensive comments and bully a student who was called a "slut" with "herpes." When Kowalski sued the school district, the Fourth Circuit court supported the school district's discipline of

DIFFERENCES BETWEEN BULLYING AND CYBERBULLYING

Bullying	Cyberbullying
Direct ⬌	**Anonymous**
Occurs on school property ⬌	**Occurs off school property**
Poor relationships with teachers ⬌	**Good relationships with teachers**
Fear retribution ⬌	**Fear loss of technology privileges**
Physical: Hitting, punching & shoving	
Verbal: Teasing, name-calling & gossip	**Further under the radar than bullying**
Nonverbal: Use of gestures & exclusion	**Emotional reactions cannot be determined**

Taken from: MaryJo Johnson, "Poll Question: Cyberbullying Legal Ramifications," Sheridan Media, October 4, 2010.

Kowalski, citing *Tinker v. Des Moines Independent Community School District* (1969), a U.S. Supreme Court case on a student's First-Amendment rights.

As established by *Tinker*, the school district successfully argued that school officials have a compelling interest in regulating speech that interferes with or disrupts the work and discipline of the school. The court in the Kowalski case determined that it was reasonably foreseeable that the speech would reach the school, so it was "satisfied that the nexus of Kowalski's speech was sufficiently strong to justify the action taken by school officials in carrying out their role as the trustees of the student body's well-being."

However, in direct contrast to the Kowalski case was the ruling in *J.C. v. Beverly Hills* [2009]. In this case a 13-year-old girl was being cyberbullied. The district tried to intervene and discipline the bully, but the courts sided with the bully and found the district violated the student's First-Amendment rights. The school district failed to meet the burden of establishing that the cyber-speech created a substantial disruption to the school environment and thus, violated the student's First-Amendment rights. As a result of the cyberbullying, administrators had to dedicate time to address the victim's concerns and the concerns of her parents, five students missed portions of classes, and the victim remained fearful of the gossip spreading. However, the courts did not consider this to be a substantial disruption.

In *J.S. v. Blue Mountain School District*, a Pennsylvania middle school student created on her home computer a spoof MySpace profile page for her principal calling him a hairy slut who hit on students, as well as other vulgar personal attacks. According to the Third Circuit Court of Appeals, the school district failed to demonstrate it could reasonably forecast that the student's words would cause substantial disruption in school, and, therefore, the student's suspension was a violation of her First Amendment right to free speech.

The companion case, *Layshock v. Hermitage School District*, also involved a Pennsylvania high school student who created a profile of his principal on MySpace that was disrespectful and lewd. The Third Circuit Court found that the school district should not have punished the student "for expressive conduct which occurred outside of the school context."

Eight education associations, including ASCA [American School Counselor Association], filed an *amici curiae* [one that is not a party to a particular litigation but is permitted to advise the court] brief with the Supreme Court explaining how school officials needed court-established standards to be able to regulate off-campus speech that in the reasonable, professional judgment of school officials interferes with maintaining a safe and effective learning environment for all students. The organizations sought, through court resolution, clarity and guidance for online conduct. In January 2012, the much-anticipated relief that was to come from the Supreme Court in the three student cyber-speech cases did not happen. The Supreme Court announced it was unwilling to accept the cases and allowed the lower courts' decisions to stand, dealing a decisive blow to educators across the country who are struggling to help victims of cyberbullying.

Educators Need a Clear Definition of Criminal Bullying

The substantial disruption test will continue to burden school officials who have the responsibility of evaluating the level of disruption occurring or that might occur on campus as a result of

Some educators believe the US Supreme Court should rule on cyberbullying in order for the nation to establish guidelines on how to deal with the problem. © Istockphoto.com/ ClarkandCompany.

off-campus online speech. School district officials are obligated under federal law to seek to remedy bullying and harassment that is severe, pervasive and objectively offensive. These statutes do not distinguish between whether bullying happened on or off campus.

School counselors do not have to decide if cyber-speech has met the criteria of substantial disruption, however. School counselors are the educators who are picking up the pieces. School counselors often receive the first outcry from students being harmed by cyber-speech and have to comfort and address students' emotional trauma. Where do we go from here? With 800 million Facebook users, more than the population of the North American continent, we have to hope the courts begin to understand that cyberbullying is about disruptive conduct and not free speech.

> "If every such breach [of a website's terms of service] does qualify [as criminal], then there is absolutely no limitation or criteria as to which of the breaches should merit criminal prosecution."

Using a Social Media Site to Create a Fake Profile for Cyberbullying Is Not Illegal

US District Court Ruling

George H. Wu

In 2006, Lori Drew, her daughter, and an employee, Ashley Grills, created a fake MySpace account for a fictitious sixteen-year-old boy, Josh Evans, for the purpose of cyberbullying a former friend of Drew's daughter. They used the profile to contact and engage in a flirtatious relationship with Megan Meier. After several months, "Josh" contacted Meier and broke off the relationship, then proceeded to send hurtful messages to the teen, suggesting that the world would be better off without her. The day these messages were sent, Meier committed suicide by hanging herself in her bedroom. No charges were brought against Drew in connection with Meier's death; however, she was charged with felony violation of the Computer Fraud and Abuse Act (CFAA). The jury in the trial found her guilty of only a misdemeanor violation of the CFAA. In

George H. Wu, *United States v. Lori Drew*, US District Court, August 28, 2009.

response, Drew filed a motion for acquittal. In the viewpoint that follows, George H. Wu, a US District Court judge, overturns the guilty verdict and finds that the grounds on which Drew was convicted were too vague. He warns that by convicting individuals for violating websites' terms of service agreements, the judicial system runs the risk of turning all Internet users into criminals, and this is not the intent of the law. George H. Wu has served as a Federal District Court judge since his appointment to the position in 2007.

During the relevant time period herein, the misdemeanor [under the Computer Fraud and Abuse Act (CFAA)] 18 U.S.C. § 1030(a)(2)(C) crime consisted of the following three elements:

> First, the defendant intentionally [accessed without authorization] [exceeded authorized access of] a computer;
>
> Second, the defendant's access of the computer involved an interstate or foreign communication; and
>
> Third, by [accessing without authorization] [exceeding authorized access to] a computer, the defendant obtained information from a computer . . . [used in interstate or foreign commerce or communication]. . . .

In this case, a central question is whether a computer user's intentional violation of one or more provisions in an Internet website's terms of services (where those terms condition access to and/or use of the website's services upon agreement to and compliance with the terms) satisfies the first element of section 1030(a)(2)(C). If the answer to that question is "yes," then seemingly, any and every conscious violation of that website's terms of service will constitute a CFAA misdemeanor. . . .

The Illegality of Actions Must Be Clearly Stated in the Law

Justice [Oliver Wendell] Holmes [Jr., who served on the US Supreme Court from 1902 to 1932] observed that, as to criminal statutes, there is a "fair warning" requirement. As he stated in *McBoyle v. United States* (1931):

> Although it is not likely that a criminal will carefully consider the text of the law before he murders or steals, it is reasonable that a fair warning should be given to the world in language that the common world will understand, of what the law intends to do if a certain line is passed. To make the warning fair, so far as possible the line should be clear. . . .

The void-for-vagueness doctrine has two prongs: 1) a definitional/notice sufficiency requirement and, more importantly, 2) a guideline setting element to govern law enforcement. In *Kolender v. Lawson* (1983), the Court explained that:

> As generally stated, the void-for-vagueness doctrine requires that a penal statute define the criminal offense with sufficient definiteness that ordinary people can understand what conduct is prohibited and in a manner that does not encourage arbitrary and discriminatory enforce-ment. . . . Although the doctrine focuses both on actual notice to citizens and arbitrary enforcement, we have recognized recently that the more important aspect of the vagueness doctrine "is not actual notice, but the other principal element of the doctrine—the requirement that a legislature establish minimal guidelines to govern law enforcement." *Smith [v. Goguen]* [1974]. Where the legislature fails to provide such minimal guidelines, a criminal statute may permit "a standardless sweep [that] allows policemen, prosecutors, and juries to pursue their personal predilections." *Id.* [Footnote and citations omitted.]

To avoid contraving the void-for-vagueness doctrine, the criminal statute must contain "relatively clear guidelines as to prohibited conduct" and provide "objective criteria" to evaluate whether a crime has been committed. *Gonzalez v. Carhart* (2007). . . .

A "difficulty in determining whether certain marginal offenses are within the meaning of the language under attack as vague does not automatically render a statute unconstitutional for indefiniteness.... Impossible standards of specificity are not required." *Jordan v. De George* (1951) (citation and footnote omitted). "What renders a statute vague is not the possibility that it will sometimes be difficult to determine whether the incriminating fact it establishes has been proved; but rather the indeterminacy of precisely what that fact is." *United States v. Williams* (2008). In this regard, the Supreme Court "has made clear that scienter requirements alleviate vagueness concerns." *Gonzales.*

"It is well established that vagueness challenges to statutes which do not involve First Amendment freedoms must be examined in the light of the facts of the case at hand." *United States v. Mazurie* (1975); *United States v. Purdy* (9th Cir. 2001). "Whether a statute is . . . unconstitutionally vague is a question of law. . . ." *United States v. Ninety-Five Firearms* (9th Cir. 1994).

Website Terms of Service Do Not Provide Sufficient Notice That a Crime Could Be Committed

The pivotal issue herein is whether basing a CFAA misdemeanor violation as per 18 U.S.C. §§ 1030(a)(2)(C) and 1030(c)(2)(A) upon the conscious violation of a website's terms of service runs afoul of the void-for-vagueness doctrine. This Court concludes that it does primarily because of the absence of minimal guidelines to govern law enforcement, but also because of actual notice deficiencies.

As discussed in Section IV(A) . . . , terms of service which are incorporated into a browsewrap or clickwrap agreement can, like any other type of contract, define the limits of authorized access as to a website and its concomitant computer/server(s). However, the question is whether individuals of "common intelligence" are on notice that a breach of a terms of service contract can become a crime under the CFAA. Arguably, they are not.

First, an initial inquiry is whether the statute, as it is written, provides sufficient notice. Here, the language of section 1030(a)

(2)(C) does not explicitly state (nor does it implicitly suggest) that the CFAA has "criminalized breaches of contract" in the context of website terms of service. Normally, breaches of contract are not the subject of criminal prosecution. Thus, while "ordinary people" might expect to be exposed to civil liabilities for violating a contractual provision, they would not expect criminal penalties. This would especially be the case where the services provided by MySpace are in essence offered at no cost to the users and, hence, there is no specter of the users "defrauding" MySpace in any monetary sense.

Breach of Vague Terms of Service Cannot Result in a Crime

Second, if a website's terms of service controls what is "authorized" and what is "exceeding authorization"—which in turn governs whether an individual's accessing information or services on the website is criminal or not, section 1030(a)(2)(C) would be unacceptably vague because it is unclear whether any or all violations of terms of service will render the access unauthorized, or whether only certain ones will. For example, in the present case, MySpace's terms of service [MSTOS] prohibits a member from engaging in a multitude of activities on the website, including such conduct as "criminal or tortious activity," "gambling," "advertising to . . . any Member to buy or sell any products," "transmit[ting] any chain letters," "covering or obscuring the banner advertisements on your personal profile page," "disclosing your password to any third party," etc. The MSTOS does not specify which precise terms of service, when breached, will result in a termination of MySpace's authorization for the visitor/member to access the website. If *any* violation of *any* term of service is held to make the access unauthorized, that strategy would probably resolve this particular vagueness issue; but it would, in turn, render the statute incredibly overbroad and contravene the second prong of the void-for-vagueness doctrine as to setting guidelines to govern law enforcement.

The daughter of Tina Meier (above) committed suicide in 2007 after being victimized by cyberbullies. In United States v. Lori Drew *(2009), a judge in the Central District of California ruled that Megan's cyberbullies did not commit a crime.* © Sarah Conard/AP Images.

Third, by utilizing violations of the terms of service as the basis for the section 1030(a)(2)(C) crime, that approach makes the website owner—in essence—the party who ultimately defines the criminal conduct. This will lead to further vagueness problems. The owner's description of a term of service might itself be so vague as to make the visitor or member reasonably unsure of what the term of service covers. For example, the MSTOS prohibits members from posting in "band and filmmaker profiles . . . sexually suggestive imagery or any other unfair . . . [c]ontent intended to draw traffic to the profile." It is unclear what "sexually suggestive imagery" and "unfair content" mean. Moreover, website owners can establish terms where either the scope or the application of the provision are to be decided by them *ad hoc* and/ or pursuant to undelineated standards. For example, the MSTOS provides that what constitutes "prohibited content" on the website is determined "in the sole discretion of MySpace.com. . . ." Additionally, terms of service may allow the website owner to unilaterally amend and/or add to the terms with minimal notice to users. . . .

The Law Cannot Be So Broad That It Turns All Internet Users into Criminals

Treating a violation of a website's terms of service, without more, to be sufficient to constitute "intentionally access[ing] a computer without authorization or exceed[ing] authorized access" would result in transforming section 1030(a)(2)(C) into an overwhelmingly overbroad enactment that would convert a multitude of otherwise innocent Internet users into misdemeanant criminals. As noted in Section IV(A) . . . , utilizing a computer to contact an Internet website by itself will automatically satisfy all remaining elements of the misdemeanor crime in 18 U.S.C. §§ 1030(a)(2)(C) and 1030(c)(2)(A). Where the website's terms of use only authorizes utilization of its services/applications upon agreement to abide by those terms (as, for example, the MSTOS does herein), any violation of any such provision can serve as a basis for finding access unauthorized and/or in excess of authorization.

One need only look to the MSTOS . . . to see the expansive and elaborate scope of such provisions whose breach engenders the potential for criminal prosecution. Obvious examples of such breadth would include: 1) the lonely-heart who submits intentionally inaccurate data about his or her age, height and/or physical appearance, which contravenes the MSTOS prohibition against providing "information that you know is false or misleading"; 2) the student who posts candid photographs of classmates without their permission, which breaches the MSTOS provision covering "a photograph of another person that you have posted without that person's consent"; and/or 3) the exasperated parent who sends out a group message to neighborhood friends en-

Cyberbullying and Parents' Liability

The primary problem with controlling cyberbullying is that cyberbullying itself is not an actionable tort [a civil wrong that causes harm to another person], nor does it fall squarely within any existing torts. Unlike the traditional bully who could be sued for assault and battery, the cyberbully only engages in hurtful speech over the Internet. Furthermore, even if the conduct was actionable under an existing tort, the child would be held to a lesser standard of care and is extremely unlikely to have saved enough of his allowance to make recovery worthwhile. Because parental immunity protects the parents from being sued for the negligent acts of their children and the Communications Decency Act (CDA) protects the Internet service providers (ISPs) from liability, plaintiffs are generally left without a remedy.

Benjamin Walther, "Cyberbullying: Holding Grownups Liable for Negligent Entrustment," Houston Law Review, *Spring 2012.*

treating them to purchase his or her daughter's girl scout cookies, which transgresses the MSTOS rule against "advertising to, or solicitation of, any Member to buy or sell any products or services through the Services." However, one need not consider hypotheticals to demonstrate the problem. In this case, Megan (who was then 13 years old) had her own profile on MySpace, which was in clear violation of the MSTOS which requires that users be "14 years of age or older." No one would seriously suggest that Megan's conduct was criminal or should be subject to criminal prosecution.

Given the incredibly broad sweep of 18 U.S.C. §§ 1030(a)(2) (C) and 1030(c)(2)(A), should conscious violations of a website's terms of service be deemed sufficient by themselves to constitute accessing without authorization or exceeding authorized access, the question arises as to whether Congress has "establish[ed] minimal guidelines to govern law enforcement." *Kolender.* Section 1030(a)(2)(C) does not set forth "clear guidelines" or "objective criteria" as to the prohibited conduct in the Internet/ website or similar contexts. For instance, section 1030(a)(2)(C) is not limited to instances where the website owner contacts law enforcement to complain about an individual's unauthorized access or exceeding permitted access on the site. Nor is there any requirement that there be any actual loss or damage suffered by the website or that there be a violation of privacy interests. . . .

Not Every Breach of Terms of Service Warrants Criminal Prosecution

Here, the Government's position is that the "intentional" requirement is met simply by a conscious violation of a website's terms of service. The problem with that view is that it basically eliminates any limiting and/or guiding effect of the scienter element. It is unclear that every intentional breach of a website's terms of service would be or should be held to be equivalent to an intent to access the site without authorization or in excess of authorization. This is especially the case with MySpace and similar Internet venues which are publically available for access and use. However, if every such breach does qualify, then there is absolutely no limitation or criteria as to which of the breaches should merit criminal prosecution. All manner of situations will be covered from the more serious (*e.g.* posting child pornography) to the more trivial (*e.g.* posting a picture of friends without their permission). All can be prosecuted. Given the "standardless sweep" that results, federal law enforcement entities would be improperly free "to pursue their personal predilections." *Kolender.*

In sum, if any conscious breach of a website's terms of service is held to be sufficient by itself to constitute intentionally accessing a computer without authorization or in excess of authorization, the result will be that section 1030(a)(2)(C) becomes a law "that affords too much discretion to the police and too little notice to citizens who wish to use the [Internet]." *City of Chicago.*

13

> "*The vacuum cleaner that would cleanse
> the Web of its pseudonymous nastiness
> would also suck up a lot of free speech.*"

The Problem with Prosecuting Cyber-Bullying

Emily Bazelon

In the viewpoint that follows, Emily Bazelon argues that many of the laws being used to prosecute cyberbullies' crimes could be detrimental to Americans' constitutional rights. Bazelon concedes that there should be a middle ground where the worst offenders are punished, but maintains that the misuse and overreach of the laws that currently exist put all Americans at risk of being prosecuted for minor cyber offenses. Emily Bazelon is a senior editor for the online magazine Slate *and a senior research fellow at Yale Law School.*

As a matter of law, the verdict against Lori Drew in the MySpace suicide case is fairly indefensible. A U.S. attorney in Los Angeles went after a misdeed in Missouri—when state and federal prosecutors there didn't think Drew's actions constituted a crime—with a crazy-broad reading of a statute written to punish computer hacking. Just about every single law professor and editorial writer to weigh in has condemned the prosecutorial overreaching. But the failure to make a valid case against Drew begs a larger question: Is there a better way to go after cyber-bullying? Or is this the kind of troublemaking, however nefarious, the government shouldn't try to punish?

Drew is the mother from hell who famously tried to defend her own teenage daughter against rumor-mongering on the Internet by creating the MySpace persona of fictional 16-year-old Josh Evans, then using that persona to fire off personal e-mail attacks (or sometimes spurring a young woman she worked with to do that). Twenty minutes after "Josh" sent 13-year-old Megan Meier, Drew's daughter's erstwhile friend, the message "the world would be a better place without you," Megan hanged herself in her bedroom.

Someone other than Drew apparently sent that last dreadful e-mail. Even if she had, it seems wrong to say she caused Megan's death. We're talking about an adolescent who must have been vulnerable and volatile and who was taking antidepressants. But the local sheriff's department's dismissal of Drew's MySpace foray as merely "rude" and "immature" doesn't seem proportionate, either. Drew was an adult who secretly entered a teenage world and made it more dangerous. A girl in that world died. The formulation that makes sense to me is that Drew at least contributed to Megan's suicide. So did the abstract verbal brutality of e-mail and the humiliation and shunning made possible by MySpace. But the vacuum cleaner that would cleanse the Web of its pseudonymous nastiness would also suck up a lot of free speech. Freedom often doesn't go with niceness.

Prosecutors Are Using Wrong Laws to Go After Bullies

The problems with the California case against Drew started with the poor fit between her wrongdoing and the law used to punish her. The federal Computer Fraud and Abuse Act [CFAA] makes it a crime to intentionally access "a computer without authorization." So what does that mean—is it a crime to hack past a password or a firewall? Or merely to violate a terms-of-service contract like the one MySpace users agree to?

In 2003, George Washington University law professor Orin Kerr wrote a prescient law-review article arguing for the former, narrower interpretation. The legislative history for the CFAA indicates that Congress wasn't trying to prosecute any or every breach of contract. Would lawmakers really want to go after people, even potentially, for giving a fake name to register for a Web site, for example (dressed up as the bad act of giving "false and misleading information")? Nor, for that matter, does it look as if Congress intended to base prison time on the MySpace contractual provision that bars use of the site that "harasses or advocates harassment of another person" or that is "abusive, threatening, obscene, defamatory, or libelous." It's one thing for MySpace to kick someone out for acting like a troll or even for the troll's target to sue her. It's another thing entirely to throw the weight of the government behind a criminal investigation and conviction for what usually just amounts to mischief in cyber-contracts.

In the Lori Drew prosecution, the theory was that Drew was on the hook for setting up the fake profile, then using it to inflict emotional distress. Three of the four counts against Drew were for "unauthorized access" of MySpace simply because Drew violated the MySpace terms of service to which she agreed, according to Los Angeles U.S. Attorney Thomas O'Brien's dubious interpretation. The jury didn't think the prosecutors proved the emotional distress and so dismissed the fourth count. And they knocked down the other charges from felonies to misdemeanors. But they did buy the idea that Drew "intentionally" broke the law, even though all that seems to mean is that she clicked "I agree" in response to a long series of legalistic paragraphs that just about nobody really reads. It's hard to imagine even these misdemeanor convictions standing up on appeal.

Lori Drew leaves a federal courthouse in Los Angeles in 2009 after a judge ruled that she did not commit a crime in an online hoax that led to the suicide of a teenage girl. Some law experts believe the prosecutors reached too far in their efforts to criminalize Drew's actions. © Nick Ut/AP Images.

Kerr joined Drew's defense team, and his post last Friday on the Volokh Conspiracy blog gets at just how ludicrous it is to imagine every breach of a Web site's terms of service as a federal crime. (Kerr: By visiting the Volokh Conspiracy, you agree that your middle name is not Ralph and that you're "super nice." You lied? Gotcha.) Of course, prosecutors aren't really going to investigate all the criminals Kerr just created with the terms of service in his post. But this is not a road we want to take even one baby step down. As Andrew Grossman argues for the Heritage

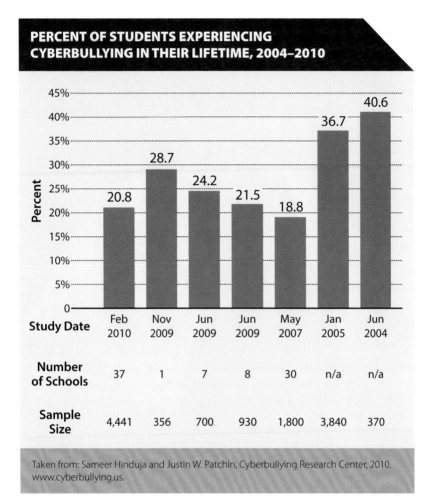

PERCENT OF STUDENTS EXPERIENCING CYBERBULLYING IN THEIR LIFETIME, 2004–2010

Study Date	Feb 2010	Nov 2009	Jun 2009	Jun 2009	May 2007	Jan 2005	Jun 2004
Percent	20.8	28.7	24.2	21.5	18.8	36.7	40.6
Number of Schools	37	1	7	8	30	n/a	n/a
Sample Size	4,441	356	700	930	1,800	3,840	370

Taken from: Sameer Hinduja and Justin W. Patchin, Cyberbullying Research Center, 2010. www.cyberbullying.us.

Foundation, laws that make it seem as if "everyone is a criminal" are generally a bad idea. Most of the time, they're unenforceable, and then every once in a while, they're used to scapegoat someone like Lori Drew.

Laws Against Cyberbullying May Even Go Too Far

What about a law written expressly to address cyber-bullying? Such a statute could presumably direct prosecutors to go after only the worst of the Internet meanies. Or, then again, maybe not. A proposed bill before Congress is far broader. It targets anyone who uses "electronic means" to transmit "in interstate or foreign commerce any communication, with the intent to coerce, intimidate, harass, or cause substantial emotional distress to a person." The penalty is a fine or imprisonment for up to two years.

Missouri, where Meier lived, has already passed a cyber-bullying law. The Missouri statute extends the state's bar on phone harassment to computers. The problem with the analogy is that the computer context is more dangerous to free speech: On the phone, you talk to one other person. On MySpace or any other Web site, you broadcast to as many people as read you. Other states have passed laws giving schools more authority to address cyber-bullying. That sounds better, but it could get schools too involved in disciplining students for the IMs and posts they write from home.

All of this takes us back to earlier battles over prosecuting hate speech. As Eugene Volokh points out on his ever-vigilant blog, the cyber-bullying bill before Congress is a classic example of a law that's unconstitutional because it's overly broad. The Supreme Court has held that the First Amendment protects "outrageous" speech—from civil as well as criminal liability— even if it "recklessly, knowingly, or purposefully causes 'severe emotional distress,' when it's about a public figure." Volokh adds, "Many, though not all, lower courts have held the same whenever the statement is on a matter of public concern, even about a private figure."

> "State-sponsored educational institutions
> may not discriminate in their
> protection of men and women based
> on a stereotype of feminine weakness or
> inferiority."

Schools Must Protect Students from Antigay Bullying

Circuit Court's Ruling

Jesse E. Eschbach

When Jamie Nabozny began middle school in the seventh grade in 1988, he recognized for the first time that he was gay. So, too, did his classmates, and Nabozny confirmed what everyone suspected by coming out as gay. As a result he was subjected to physical and emotional bullying at the hands of his classmates through middle and high school, with limited to no disciplinary action taken by school administrators. Eventually, Nabozny withdrew from high school in the eleventh grade and in 1995 sued the administrators who failed to offer him protection, claiming they violated his Fourteenth Amendment rights of equal protection and due process. After a district court ruled against Nabozny, the suit moved to the US Court of Appeals, Seventh Circuit. The following viewpoint presents the ruling of Judge Jesse E. Eschbach, who found

Jesse E. Eschbach, *Nabozny v. Podlesny*, US Circuit Court, July 31, 1996.

that the schools' failure to take action against Nabozny's bullies resulted from Nabozny's gender and sexual orientation, and thus constituted discrimination. Eschbach determined that the evidence presented by Nabozny and the school officials confirmed that had the same type of abuse happened to female students, immediate action to stop it would have been taken. Thus, he concluded that the school's failure stemmed directly from discriminatory views regarding Nabozny's gender and homosexuality. Jesse E. Eschbach served as a federal judge from 1962 until his retirement in 2000.

Jamie Nabozny was a student in the Ashland Public School District (hereinafter "the District") in Ashland, Wisconsin throughout his middle school and high school years. During that time, Nabozny was continually harassed and physically abused by fellow students because he is homosexual. Both in middle school and high school Nabozny reported the harassment to school administrators. Nabozny asked the school officials to protect him and to punish his assailants. Despite the fact that the school administrators had a policy of investigating and punishing student-on-student battery and sexual harassment, they allegedly turned a deaf ear to Nabozny's requests. Indeed, there is evidence to suggest that some of the administrators themselves mocked Nabozny's predicament. Nabozny eventually filed suit against several school officials and the District pursuant to 42 U.S.C. Section 1983 alleging, among other things, that the defendants: 1) violated his Fourteenth Amendment right to equal protection by discriminating against him based on his gender; 2) violated his Fourteenth Amendment right to equal protection by discriminating against him based on his sexual orientation; 3) violated his Fourteenth Amendment right to due process by exacerbating the risk that he would be harmed by fellow students; and, 4) violated his Fourteenth Amendment right to due process by encouraging an environment in which he would be harmed. The defendants filed a motion for summary judgment, which the district court granted. Nabozny appeals the district court's decision. Because we agree with the district court only in part, we affirm in part, reverse in part, and remand. . . .

Schools Must Offer Equal Protection to All Their Students

We will begin our analysis by considering Nabozny's equal protection claims, reserving Nabozny's due process claims for subsequent treatment in the opinion. Wisconsin has elected to protect the students in its schools from discrimination. [A] Wisconsin statute section regulating general school operations, provides that:

> No person may be denied . . . participation in, be denied the benefits of or be discriminated against in any curricular, extracurricular, pupil services, recreational or other program or activity because of the person's sex, race, religion, national origin, ancestry, creed, pregnancy, marital or parental status, sexual orientation or physical, mental, emotional or learning disability.

Since at least 1988, in compliance with the state statute, the Ashland Public School District has had a policy of prohibiting discrimination against students on the basis of gender or sexual orientation. The District's policy and practice includes protecting students from student-on-student sexual harassment and battery. Nabozny maintains that the defendants denied him the equal protection of the law by denying him the protection extended to other students, based on his gender and sexual orientation.

The Equal Protection Clause grants to all Americans "the right to be free from invidious discrimination in statutory classifications and other governmental activity." *Harris v. McRae* (1980). When a state actor turns a blind eye to the Clause's command, aggrieved parties such as Nabozny can seek relief pursuant to 42 U.S.C. Section 1983. In order to establish liability under Section 1983, Nabozny must show that the defendants acted with a nefarious discriminatory purpose, *Personnel Adm'r of Massachusetts v. Feeney* (1979), and discriminated against him based on his membership in a definable class. *Albright v. Oliver* (7th Cir. 1992). As we explained in *Shango v. Jurich* (7th Cir. 1982):

> The gravamen of equal protection lies not in the fact of deprivation of a right but in the invidious classification of persons aggrieved by the state's action. A plaintiff must demonstrate intentional or purposeful discrimination to show an equal protection violation. Discriminatory purpose, however, implies more than intent as volition or intent as awareness of consequences. It implies that a decisionmaker singled out a particular group for disparate treatment and selected his course of action at least in part for the purpose of causing its adverse effects on the identifiable group.

A showing that the defendants were negligent will not suffice. Nabozny must show that the defendants acted either intentionally or with deliberate indifference. To escape liability, the defendants either must prove that they did not discriminate against Nabozny, or at a bare minimum, the defendants' discriminatory conduct must satisfy one of two well-established standards of review: heightened scrutiny in the case of gender discrimination, or rational basis in the case of sexual orientation.

The district court found that Nabozny had proffered no evidence to support his equal protection claims. In the alternative, the court granted to the defendants qualified immunity. Considering the facts in the light most favorable to Nabozny, we respectfully disagree with the district court's conclusions.

Schools Cannot Discriminate Based on Gender

The district court disposed of Nabozny's equal protection claims in two brief paragraphs. Regarding the merits of Nabozny's gender claim, the court concluded that "there is absolutely nothing in the record to indicate that plaintiff was treated differently because of his gender." The district court's conclusion affords two interpretations: 1) there is no evidence that the defendants treated Nabozny differently from other students; or, 2) there is no evidence that the discriminatory treatment was based on Nabozny's gender. We will examine each in turn.

The record viewed in the light most favorable to Nabozny, combined with the defendants' own admissions, suggests that Nabozny was treated differently from other students. The defendants stipulate that they had a commendable record of enforcing their anti-harassment policies. Yet Nabozny has presented evidence that his classmates harassed and battered him for years and that school administrators failed to enforce their anti-harassment policies, despite his repeated pleas for them to do so. If the defendants otherwise enforced their anti-harassment policies, as they contend, then Nabozny's evidence strongly suggests that they made an exception to their normal practice in Nabozny's case.

Therefore, the question becomes whether Nabozny can show that he received different treatment because of his gender. Nabozny's evidence regarding the defendants' punishment of male-on-female battery and harassment is not overwhelming. Nabozny contends that a male student that struck his girlfriend was immediately expelled, that males were reprimanded for striking girls, and that when pregnant girls were called "slut" or "whore," the school took action. Nabozny's evidence does not include specific facts, such as the names and dates of the individuals involved. Nabozny does allege, however, that when he was subjected to a mock rape [Ashland Middle School principal Mary] Podlesny responded by saying "boys will be boys," apparently dismissing the incident because both the perpetrators and the victim were males. We find it impossible to believe that a female lodging a similar complaint would have received the same response.

More important, the defendants do not deny that they aggressively punished male-on-female battery and harassment.

LGBT Students Face Barriers to Holding Schools Accountable for Discrimination

Students who experience discriminatory policies or customs and wish to bring equal protection claims against towns or school districts may face a host of social and legal barriers. As an initial matter, students might be reluctant to report harassment to teachers, school officials, or school district administrators. LGBT [lesbian, gay, bisexual, and transgender] students might be particularly reluctant to draw attention to their sexual orientation if they live in an area where residents view their sexual orientation or gender identity as shameful. Even students and families who are willing to sue might not have sufficient knowledge about other students' bullying experiences to claim that the school district treats some victims of bullying differently from others. Because school districts and their employees do not have a general duty under federal law to protect students from one another's abuse, they will only be found liable when students can show that school districts responded differently to LGBT bullying than to non-LGBT bullying. Finally, even when students can show that LGBT bullied students were treated differently than non-LGBT bullied students, the students still may not be able to overcome school administrators' immunity defenses, or be able to prove that the school districts were aware of the bullying.

Yariv Pierce, "Put the Town on Notice: School District Liability and LGBT Bullying Notification Laws," University of Michigan Journal of Law Reform, Fall 2012.

The defendants argue that they investigated and punished all complaints of battery and harassment, regardless of the victim's gender. According to the defendants, contrary to the evidence presented by Nabozny, they aggressively pursued each of Nabozny's complaints and punished the alleged perpetrators whenever possible. Like Nabozny, the defendants presented evidence to support their claim. Whether to believe the defendants or Nabozny is, of course, a question of credibility for the fact-finder. In the context of considering the defendants' summary judgment motion, we must assume that Nabozny's version is the credible one. If Nabozny's evidence is considered credible, the record taken in conjunction with the defendants' admissions demonstrates that the defendants treated male and female victims differently.

The defendants also argue that there is no evidence that they either intentionally discriminated against Nabozny, or were deliberately indifferent to his complaints. The defendants concede that they had a policy and practice of punishing perpetrators of battery and harassment. It is well settled law that departures from established practices may evince discriminatory intent. *Village of Arlington Heights v. Metropolitan Housing Dev. Corp.* (1977). Moreover, Nabozny introduced evidence to suggest that the defendants literally laughed at Nabozny's pleas for help. The defendants' argument, considered against Nabozny's evidence, is simply indefensible.

Gender Stereotypes Must Not Lead to Discrimination

Our inquiry into Nabozny's gender equal protection claim does not end here, because the district court granted to the defendants qualified immunity. The District itself clearly is not entitled to qualified immunity. Therefore, we need only consider whether the individual defendants are immune from suit.

In *Harlow v. Fitzgerald* (1982), the Supreme Court held that "government officials performing discretionary functions generally are shielded from liability for civil damages insofar as their conduct does not violate clearly established statutory or constitutional rights of which a reasonable person would have known." If the law was not "clearly established," no liability should result because "an official could not reasonably be expected to anticipate subsequent legal developments, nor could be said to 'know' that the law forbade conduct not previously identified as unlawful." Thus, the critical questions in this case are whether the law "clearly establishes" the basis for Nabozny's claim, and whether the law was so established in 1988 when Nabozny entered middle school. *Sherman v. Four County Counseling Ctr.* (7th Cir. 1993).

The Fourteenth Amendment provides that a State shall not "deny to any person within its jurisdiction the equal protection of the laws." In 1971, the Supreme Court interpreted the Equal Protection Clause to prevent arbitrary gender-based discrimination. A few years later, in *Weinberger v. Wiesenfeld* (1975), the Court held that discrimination based on "gender-based generalizations" in society runs afoul of the Equal Protection Clause.

In *Mississippi University for Women v. Hogan* (1982), building on its earlier precedents, the Court went further in requiring equal treatment regardless of gender. In *Hogan*, the Court struck down a state statute that prevented males from enrolling in a state nursing school as violating the Equal Protection Clause. Rejecting Mississippi's argument that gender-biased enrollment criteria were necessary to compensate for prior discrimination, the Court held that "if the statutory objective is to exclude or 'protect' members of one gender because they are presumed to suffer from an inherent handicap or to be innately inferior, the objective itself is illegitimate." *Hogan* made clear, in 1982, that state-sponsored educational institutions may not discriminate in their protection of men and women based on a stereotype of feminine weakness or inferiority. It is now well settled that to survive constitutional scrutiny, gender based discrimination must be substantially related to an important governmental objective.

Equal Protection Does Not Mean Identical Treatment for Everyone

Nonetheless, the defendants ask us to affirm the grant of qualified immunity because "there was no clear duty under the equal

Jamie Nabozny stands in the hall of the high school where he was subjected to antigay bullying. In Nabozny v. Podlesny *(1996), the Seventh Circuit Court of Appeals ruled that the school administrators' failure to protect Nabozny stemmed directly from their discriminatory views regarding his sexual orientation.* © Taro Yamasaki//Time Life Pictures/Getty Images.

protection clause for the individual defendants to enforce every student complaint of harassment by other students the same way." The defendants are correct in that the Equal Protection Clause does not require the government to give everyone identical treatment. Nothing we say today suggests anything to the contrary. The Equal Protection Clause does, however, require the state to treat each person with equal regard, as having equal worth, regardless of his or her status. The defendants' argument fails because they frame their inquiry too narrowly. The question is not whether they are required to treat every harassment complaint the same way; as we have noted, they are not. The question is whether they are required to give male and female students equivalent levels of protection; they are, absent an important governmental objective, and the law clearly said so prior to Nabozny's years in middle school.

The defendants bemoan the fact that there is no prior case directly on point with facts identical to this case. Under the doctrine of qualified immunity, liability is not predicated upon the existence of a prior case that is directly on point. The question is whether a reasonable state actor would have known that his actions, viewed in the light of the law at the time, were unlawful. We believe that reasonable persons standing in the defendants' shoes at the time would have reached just such a conclusion. . . .

Equal Protection Must Not Be Denied Based on Gender or Sexual Orientation

We conclude that, based on the record as a whole, a reasonable fact-finder could find that the District and defendants Podlesny, [Ashland High School principal William Davis and assistant principal Thomas Blauert] violated Nabozny's Fourteenth Amendment right to equal protection by discriminating against him based on his gender or sexual orientation. Further, the law establishing the defendants' liability was sufficiently clear to inform the defendants at the time that their conduct was unconstitutional. Nabozny's equal protection claims against the District, Podlesny, Davis, and Blauert are reinstated in toto.

> *"Laws against insulting people's groups teach us that we should get upset when people insult our groups. And when we get upset, the problem gets worse."*

The Solution to "Gay" Insults: Freedom of Speech

Izzy Kalman

In the viewpoint that follows, Izzy Kalman, a nationally certified school psychologist, argues that the laws making antigay speech illegal infringe on free speech rights and intensify existing hatred and resentment of the gay community and the individuals within it. As a result, Kalman maintains that antigay bullying will only worsen with the implementation of new laws to outlaw insults against people who are gay. The solution to the antigay bullying, in the author's view, is not enacting new laws to make antigay speech illegal, but using free speech to counter bullies' false claims. Kalman suggests that people who encounter prejudiced individuals should engage them in conversation and use the interaction as an opportunity to combat their negative views. Izzy Kalman has worked as a school psychologist since 1978 with a focus on how to stop bullying from a psychological perspective.

There was a recent high profile story in the news about an 11-year old boy who committed suicide, apparently because he could no longer tolerate being called "gay." Sadly, this story is not unusual. The highest suicide rate of all groups is said to be among gays. What was unusual in the recent incident is the young age of the person who committed the act.

The most common insult among kids today is "gay." It is used not only to mean "someone who is attracted to people of his/her own gender," but as a synonym for "stupid" or "bad." Kids get mad when they are called gay and they sometimes get into fights.

I have great compassion for gays. Not only do they have to deal with the derision and even hatred of a large proportion of the general public, they also need to deal with their own angst about being different.

What is one to do when called gay? The anti-bully movement is trying to solve the problem by passing laws making it illegal to insult anyone. Many anti-bully activists insist that anti-bully laws should *specifically* mention insults against gays and those of non-heterosexual orientations. If it becomes a crime to insult people, then, it is hoped, no one will be attacked with the "gay" insult, and the associated violence will disappear.

One of the problems with making it illegal to call someone "gay" is that it violates the First Amendment right to Freedom of Speech. However, few people today understand and value Freedom of Speech. Most people seem to believe that it is worth getting rid of Freedom of Speech in order to protect people's feelings.

The truth is that society has come a long way in recent decades toward reducing hatred and discrimination against gays. However, it will be a while—*if ever*—before anti-gay sentiment disappears *completely*. So what is one to do when called gay? If it is happening to you, and you need to wait till prejudice disappears from the face of the earth, your problem may never end. Using laws to punish people for using "gay" as an insult is not likely to solve the problem, either. If people get punished for insulting

gays, do you think they are going to think, "Now I respect gays so much because they got me punished"? Of course not! They are going to hate gays even more, and think they are big crybabies who need the help of the government.

Fortunately, as I routinely demonstrate through role-playing at my seminars, the solution to this problem that has hurt so many people is remarkably simple. We can deal with gay insults all by ourselves, and at the same time help reduce prejudice in society. As I will be showing, Freedom of Speech is not the *cause* of the problem but the *solution*! And it is mandated by the Golden Rule, which is the ultimate solution to interpersonal problems. Few people are aware of it, but the Golden Rule really comes to teach us that we need to treat people like friends even when they treat us like enemies.

Of course, the following dialogues are imaginary, and the age and sophistication of the kids involved will determine the content of the dialogues in real life. So please don't get caught up with the specific words; it is the *attitudes* that matter. And the gender of the people is also not relevant. But since I am a male, it is easier for me to write the scripts as though I am a male. (And when I identify the insulter as "You," I don't mean *you*, the reader, of course. It's just easy to write the scenes this way, as a dialogue between "Me" and "You.")

Scenario Number One: I am *not* gay, but you call me gay.

You: You are soooo gay!

Me: No, I'm not!

You: Yes, you are! Everyone knows you're gay!

Me: How can they know something that's not true?

You: Didn't you ever look in the mirror? You're *flaming* gay!

Me: No, I'm not! Stop calling me gay!

You: Why should I stop? I'm going to keep on calling you gay until you admit it's true!

Me: But it's not true! Shut your mouth already or I'll shut it for you!

You: A little fairy like you! Hah! How are you going to shut my mouth?

Me: I will! You call me gay one more time and I'll have no choice!

You: Gay, gay, gay, gay, gay! Go ahead! Try and stop me!

This, of course, will lead to nowhere but a fight. Now I'll respond differently. I will give you Freedom of Speech and treat you like a friend.

You: You are soooo gay!

Me: How come you think I'm gay?

You: Just look in the mirror and you'll see.

Me: I do look in the mirror. What about me do you think makes me look gay?

You: The way you dress. Those pants are so tight. Only gays would wear pants like that.

Me: They are 50's style. Marlon Brando and James Dean used to wear pants like that.

You: Well, they must have been gay.

Me: I don't think so. I think they were really hot with the women.

You: They were?

Me: Yeah! You should watch some of their movies. They're real classics.

You: Only gays like old movies.

Me: Oh, you'd be surprised. You should watch, *On The Waterfront* and *Rebel Without a Cause.* You'd love them.

You: Well, maybe I'll watch them sometime.

Me: You won't regret it!

You: Thanks.

Much better, isn't it. And it was so easy. I just treated you like a friend and told myself you have the right to say whatever you want.

Scenario Number Two: I *am* gay and have "come out," and you hate gays with a passion. Let's say we are in high school, because by that age we are likely to be aware of our true sexual orientation.

You: You know, you are going to burn in hell!

Me: No, I'm not!

You: Yes, you will! The Bible says all gays are going to burn in hell!

Me: The Bible is nonsense! It was written by homophobic men!

You: No, it wasn't! God wrote the Bible and it says you are going to suffer eternal damnation!

Me: No, I won't! You're the one who's going to burn in hell because God hates bigots!

You: God loves *me*! He hates *you*! That's why he sent AIDS to kill you off!

Me: How dare you talk to me like that? You are violating my civil rights!

You: Oh, yeah? What are you going to do? Call the police?

Me: Maybe I should!

You: Yeah, go ahead, you gay sissy! Guess what? The police hate gays, too! They're not going to help you!

Me: Yes, they will! It's the law!

After two local hate crimes occurred in 2010, gay activists participated in Queer Rising's Take Back the Night march in New York City. Some argue that engaging the community in conversation about antigay attitudes is a better solution than enacting laws. © Yana Paskova/ Getty Images.

You: Hah, hah! No law can help you! Gays are beyond help!

Me: Shut your mouth already!

Again, this goes nowhere except endless hostility.
This time I'll give you Freedom of Speech and treat you like a friend.

You: You know, you are going to burn in hell!

Me: Why do you say that?

You: Because you are gay!

Me: And you think gays are going to hell?

You: Yes! The Bible says so!

Me: Well, I sure hope it's not true.

You: It is!

Me: How do you know?

You: I told you already. The Bible says so. And that's what my priest says, too!

Me: Yes, a lot of priests say that. You know, there were a lot of stories in the news about priests molesting young boys. Does that mean they are gay, too?

You: I guess so.

Me: Will they go to hell, too?

You: Sure.

Me: Boy, I'm sure glad there will be some priests to confess to in hell!

You: Stop kidding around. I mean it. You are going to go to hell if you stay gay.

Me: Why do you think it is so terrible to be gay?

You: Because the Bible says "Adam and *Eve*," not, "Adam and *Steve*."

Me: If God didn't want there to be gays, why did he make me gay?

You: He didn't make you gay. You *chose* to be gay!

Me: You think I *chose* to be gay?

You: Of course. Everyone knows it's a choice.

Me: Are you *straight?*

You: Of course!

Me: Do you remember *choosing* to be straight?

You: I didn't have to choose. I was *born* straight.

Me: That's right. You didn't choose to be straight. You never had to ask yourself, "Should I be straight, or should I be gay?

I think I'll be straight!" Well, you know what, I never chose, either. If it were a choice, do you think I would have chosen to be gay?

You: Well, you obviously did!

Me: Believe me, if it were a choice, I would have chosen to be straight. You know how tough it is to be gay?

You: No.

Me: Oh, it's a bummer! People hate you just for what you are. They treat you like a freak and tell you you're going to hell. When I first realized I was gay, I thought, "Oh, no. What am I going to do? People are going to hate me. How am I going to live a normal life? And how am I going to tell my parents?" Believe me, if it were a choice, I would have picked straight.

You: Well, it's not too late! You can still choose to become straight.

Me: Believe me, I tried. I went out with girls. I figured, if I go out with enough girls, I'd learn to be attracted to them. But it didn't work. I mean, I love their company. We have so much in common. But I was never attracted to them.

You: Maybe you didn't go out with the right girl.

Me: Dude, it's nice that you care so much about me, but believe me, I went out with the "right" girls. But it didn't help. I just had to become cool with the fact that I'm gay, and then I became happier.

You: I think you should still try anyway. In my church, they run this program that turns gay people straight.

Me: I went to a program like that for a whole year. All it did was make me feel guilty. It didn't make me straight.

You: Well, maybe the program in my church is better. You should try it.

Me: Thanks again for wanting to help me. I really appreciate it. But I'm gay, and I'm okay with it now.

You: Well, if that's what makes you happy . . .

Me: Yes, it does. Thanks for the concern.

You: You're welcome.

Obviously much better this time. If we go to school together, are in the same classes, and I always treat you this way, you may even become my friend even though you hate gays. And you may even end up thinking, "Well, maybe gays aren't that bad after all." So why do I need the government's help with this? I can turn you into a less prejudiced person all by myself if I give you Freedom of Speech and treat you like a friend. . . .

Scenario Number Three: I suspect that I am gay, and I look gay. However, I'm not ready to "come out." The idea that I may be gay disturbs me and I don't want to admit that I am unsure about my sexual orientation.

You: You are soooo gay!

Me: No, I'm not!

You: Yes, you are! It is so obvious!

Me: No it's not! And I'm not gay!

You: Man, you really have blinders. Haven't you looked in the mirror? It is so obvious that you are gay!

Me: I am not gay! Stop saying that I look gay!

You: But it's so obvious that you are! You know, you are going to be the last person in the world to know that you are gay!

Me: No I won't! Because I'm not!

You: Oh, my God! You are so clueless! Everyone knows you are gay.

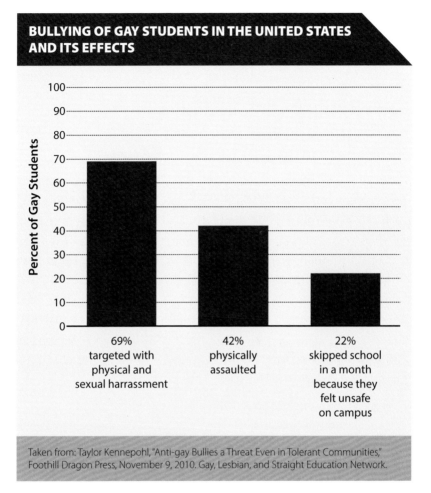

BULLYING OF GAY STUDENTS IN THE UNITED STATES AND ITS EFFECTS

Percent of Gay Students

69% targeted with physical and sexual harrassment

42% physically assaulted

22% skipped school in a month because they felt unsafe on campus

Taken from: Taylor Kennepohl, "Anti-gay Bullies a Threat Even in Tolerant Communities," Foothill Dragon Press, November 9, 2010. Gay, Lesbian, and Straight Education Network.

Me: No, I'm not!

This, of course, gets me nowhere. Now I'll do it the better way.

You: You are soooo gay!

Me: Why do you say that?

You: Because you look gay. It's so obvious. Look in the mirror.

Me: You know what? You are not the first person who told me they think I'm gay.

You: Duh! If it has feathers, isn't it a bird?

Me: I know I'm not the most macho guy in the world.

You: You can say that again!

Me: So you actually think I'm gay?

You: Yes. Aren't you?

Me: No. But I know that some people think I am.

You: Yes, they do!

Me: Yes, they do.

It pretty much fizzles out here, and you will leave me alone. You will stop trying to torment me by calling me gay because it doesn't bother me. And you will respect me more because I am showing you respect, and I am not making a fool out of myself.

Scenario Number Four: I'm *not* gay, but you are going to tell me you heard a rumor that I am.

You: You know, Johnny said that you're gay! He said he saw you kissing another guy!

Me: No I didn't!

You: Johnny doesn't lie. You're gay!

Me: No, I'm not!

You: Don't try to deny it! You were kissing a guy, and that means you are gay!

Me: I'm not gay! And I don't kiss guys!

You (in a sing-song voice): Hah, hah! Izzy i-is ga-ay, Izzy i-is ga-ay!

Me: Shut your mouth! I am not gay!

You (singing): Yes, you-ou a-are! You a-are ga-ay! Izzy is a faggot! Ha, ha ha *ha* ha!

Me: Shut your mouth!!!

Of course I'm a big loser here and you are going to keep on tormenting me. Now we'll do it again.

You: You know, Johnny said that you're gay! He said he saw you kissing another guy!

Me: Do you believe him?

You: Yes!

Me: If you want to believe him, I can't stop you.

You: No, you can't.

Me: That's right. I can't.

And that's usually where it ends.

When you come to tell me this rumor, you want to see me defending myself. But it's a trap. I automatically lose by defending myself because it is the weaker position. Since all living creatures are programmed to try to win, you are going to keep on attacking me with this rumor to get me to defend myself.

So the second time, instead of defending myself from the rumor, I turned the tables on you. I made you defend *yourself* by asking you, *"Do you believe it?"* Now you have to decide if you want to acknowledge believing a rumor about me. If you say you believe it, I say, "You can believe it if you want," and I come out being the winner. And if you say you *don't* believe it, I also win. So don't defend yourself from rumors. Just ask the person, "Do you believe it?" and you come out being the winner. . . .

Scenario Number Five: I'm not gay, and you come to tell me that other people are spreading a rumor that I am.

You: You know, everyone is saying that you're gay!

Me: I can't believe it! Who's saying it?

You: Everybody! The whole school is saying that you're gay!

Me: That's terrible! You have to tell them it's not true!

You: How do I know it isn't? If everyone's saying it, it must be true!

Me: It's not true! I swear it! I am not gay! You have to tell them to stop!

You: I can't make them stop. There are too many of them. Anyway, how do I know it's not true?

Me: I swear I am not gay! You have to help me stop them from saying it! How can I come to school if everyone thinks I'm gay?

This is obviously not working. Now we'll do it again, and I'll use Freedom of Speech.

You: You know, everyone is saying that you're gay!

Me: Really? That's what they're saying?

You: Yes. That's the word going around the whole school!

Me: Well, if they want to say it, I can't stop them.

You: But how can you let them get away with it? You can't let everyone call you gay!

Me: I can't stop them. People have a right to say whatever they want.

You: You mean it doesn't bother you that everyone's saying you're gay?

Me: I'd rather they didn't, but if they want to do it, I can't stop them.

You: Dude, you're weird! But you're cool!

Me: Thanks.

Scenario Number Six: I'm gay and I've "come out." You come to tell me that you heard I'm gay.

You: You know, I heard you're gay!

Me: Yes, I am, and I'm proud of it!

You: Wow, you're a *faggot*!

Me: Don't call me a faggot! The word is *gay*!

You: I can't believe it! You really are a faggot! You're a freak!

Me: The word is *gay*! And I'm not a freak!

You: Yes, you are! All gays are freaks!

Me: We are not freaks! There is nothing wrong with being gay!

You: Yes there is! Everyone knows that gays are freaks!

Me: No, we're not! Shut your mouth!

Again, I'm a big loser. You are going to keep on tormenting me, and you are not going to have respect either for me or for gay people in general. This time I'll handle it better.

You: You know, I heard you're gay!

Me: Oh! You just found out?

You: Yes! You mean you actually are gay?

Me: Yes. I thought everyone knew.

You: Well, *I* didn't.

Me: So now you know, too.

[*The situation could end here. I may also want to use the opportunity for a "teaching moment," so I'll ask you:*] How do you feel about gays?

You: I think they're freaks.

Me: A lot of people do. Why do you think we are freaks?

You: It's gross! Guys "doing it" with guys! You are supposed to "do it" with girls.

Me: Well, it works that way for most people, but not if you're gay.

You: It really grosses me out thinking about two guys "doing it" with each other.

Me: Well, that's exactly the way I feel when I think of a guy and a girl "doing it" together.

You: You do?

Me: Yep!

You: Boy, you're weird!

Me: To straight people, gays seem weird.

You: They sure do.

Me: And to us, straight people seem weird.

You: Boy, it's a strange world!

Me: It sure is!

So you see, by treating you like a friend and giving you Freedom of Speech, you will end up having more respect and understanding for both my group and myself, and you may end up becoming my friend. And you will certainly stop trying to torment me for being gay because your efforts to torment me won't work. . . .

Scenario Number Seven: Young kids calling each other gay.

This is the final scenario I'll be presenting here. Young kids today also use gay as an insult. They may not know their own true sexual orientation yet, and they may not even know the sexual meaning of the word "gay."

You: You are sooo gay!

Me: No, I'm not!

You: Yes, you are!

Me: Stop calling me gay! I am not gay!

You: Yes you are:

Me: No, I'm not! Stop calling me gay!

You: Gay gay gay gay gay!

Me: Stop it!

You: Gay gay gay gay gay!

Me: Stop!!!

I'm a big loser this way. We'll do it again and I'll treat you like a friend.

You: You are sooo gay!

Me: What does that mean?

You: You are stupid.

Me: Why do you think I'm stupid?

You: Well, you didn't even know what "gay" means.

Me: You're right. I hear the word so much but I wasn't really sure. Is that all it means—stupid?

You: Yes. It means "stupid."

Me: Thanks for letting me know.

You: You're welcome.

And it's over!

So you see, we don't need laws or other people's protection to stop people from calling us gay. In fact, these laws against insulting people's groups teach us that we *should* get upset when people insult our groups. And when we get upset, the problem gets *worse*.

All we need is to learn the practice of the Golden Rule, which really means that we should treat people like friends even when they treat us like enemies. And Freedom of Speech is *mandated* by the Golden Rule.

Note: Please don't complain to me, "But we need these laws! Attacks against gays aren't only verbal! There are physical attacks, and we are victims of discrimination, too!"

Yes, of course there are physical attacks and real discrimination against gays. But these acts are *already* crimes, and rightfully so, and they have nothing to do with Freedom of Speech. Freedom of Speech only guarantees people's right to say words that can hurt our feelings, but it does not give them the right to hurt our bodies or possessions, to deny members of our groups equal opportunity, to treat us differently under the law, to threaten us, or to incite violence against us. Furthermore, most physical attacks *begin* with words, so if we know how to successfully handle verbal attacks against our group, there will probably be no escalation to physical attacks.

It is not more *laws* that we need, but more *education*. We need to teach the meaning and practice of Freedom of Speech and the Golden Rule.

By the way, a few years ago I wrote a series of articles showing how to use my "Bullies to Buddies" rules to solve the problem of prejudice, using anti-Semitism as the example. I have recently edited these into a manual called *The Golden Rule Solution to Racism*. If you think it is worthwhile, please feel free to send the link to others, too. The link is here: http://www.bullies2buddies.com/How-to-Stop-Racism

And don't forget all the other valuable info that is to be found on www.Bullies2Buddies.com!

> "I had returned to Lutterworth College,
> not as a damaged ex-pupil seeking
> closure, but as a fellow school leader."

A Man Describes How He Overcame Antigay Bullying and Helps Students Deal with It Today

Personal Narrative

Shaun Dellenty

In this personal narrative, Shaun Dellenty tells the story of how he was bullied in school for being gay, quit school, but then returned to the school as an adult to educate students about bullying. Dellenty says that he hated attending the school where he was picked on and humiliated and that neither educators nor his parents knew how to help. Later, as an adult and school leader, Dellenty was able to return to that school to train students on diversity and offer them his personal story of triumph. Shaun Dellenty is deputy head at Alfred Salter Primary School in London. In 2010, he started the Inclusion for All initiative to address bullying in his school.

The last time I walked out of Lutterworth grammar school, back in 1987, I nearly gave up on my future.

Years of sustained homophobic bullying from pupils in and around school meant that all signs pointed to an unhappy exit from planet Earth at the earliest opportunity; a feeling compounded by the fact that my parents had recently discovered the truth behind the graffiti that was scrawled all over the town. I was gay.

My parents' reaction, in a genuine attempt to do the right thing, was to announce they were going to book me in for electro convulsion and psychotherapy.

But my feelings of anxiety and depression were so deep rooted that I was sticking knives into my arms and exploring ways of ending my own existence. School at the time meant rejection, dread and humiliation. Despite studying for my A levels [qualification test for entrance into university in the United Kingdom], I was becoming a non-attender. So I was called to the head of sixth form. He asked me why I had missed lessons. For the first time, authenticity seemed the best option.

"I'm gay, and I'm having a terrible time."

"Oh I see," he said pushing his chair backwards.

"Sometimes I think it would be better if I just left."

"Yes, well perhaps that would be for the best."

And with that I began my walk towards the school gate and an uncertain future. In the intervening years I fought hard to see the bigger picture and never to give up on life, hope and education. Decades passed, Aids wiped out a generation of young people, wars were won, ages of consent were lowered, and perhaps, one day soon, I will be free to marry someone because I love them.

Victims of Bullying Can Educate Others About Bullying

Two weeks ago [July 2013], by invitation, I walked back into the school I had walked out of: Lutterworth grammar school, now Lutterworth College.

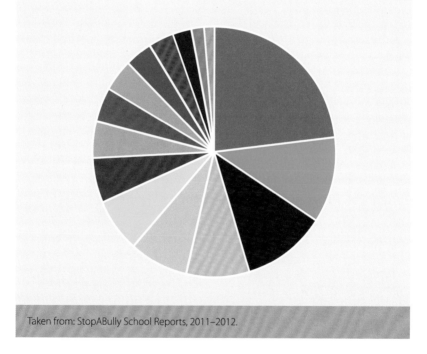

TYPES OF BULLYING REPORTED IN CANADIAN SCHOOLS, SEPTEMBER 2011 TO APRIL 2012

Name Calling / Insults (80%)

Shoving / Hitting (39%)

Threats / Intimidation (38%)

Spreading Rumors (29%)

Cyberbullying (27%)

Involving Friends / Peers (24%)

Homophobic Comments (20%)

Fighting (16%)

Sexual Comments (16%)

Exclusion / Leaving Out (14%)

Cell Phone Messages (13%)

Racist Comments (11%)

Damaging Property (9%)

Stealing (6%)

Weapon Related (4%)

Taken from: StopABully School Reports, 2011–2012.

I found myself back in my old maths block, accompanied by one of my old—but seemingly not older—teachers to talk to pupils about my experiences as part of the first ever Lutterworth College diversity day.

Lutterworth is a small market town in middle England, which despite being only 20 miles from Leicester, seems wrapped in the same small-town shroud of limited perspectives that it was in 1987. This inaugural diversity day provided students with information on people living with HIV, religions and disabilities, practical activities to develop a range of cultural skills, and a workshop looking at the tragic case of Sophie Lancaster, the student who was beaten to death for being a goth.

Lutterworth College principal Andrew Cooper told me that, despite living close to Leicester, one of the most vibrant and culturally diverse cities in the country, many students come to the college with a limited understanding of cultural diversity. The day was one way of helping to address that.

But other important diversity work has been going on at the college and a recent Ofsted [Office for Standards in Education, Children's Services and Skills, Great Britain's official body for inspecting schools] report judged that the college had a "good understanding of problems caused by various forms of discriminations, for example racism and homophobia."

At my own school, Alfred Salter primary, in December 2012 Ofsted found our anti-homophobia work to be "outstanding." These are clear signs that Ofsted regards preventing homophobic bullying as a high priority. Other schools please take note.

Some Things Change for the Better

I had returned to Lutterworth College, not as a damaged ex-pupil seeking closure, but as a fellow school leader. I found a much improved organisation. Since confirming to my own school community that I'm gay and had been bullied, I have founded a charitable organisation called Inclusion for All. I now train other teachers to help prevent homophobic bullying.

The audience for my final session of the day was all boys. They listened intently as I outlined the damage that using the word gay pejoratively [as a derogatory term] can cause. As the final bell rang, a few boys approached me.

"We wanted to shake your hand, sir—you've inspired us. We have been doing this kind of bad stuff and wanted to say thanks."

Three hours later I received a tweet: "Thank you sir, you've changed my life."

As I walked out of Lutterworth College in 2013, I felt proud of them and proud for them.

Organizations to Contact

The editors have compiled the following list of organizations concerned with the issues debated in this book. The descriptions are derived from materials provided by the organizations. All have publications or information available for interested readers. The list was compiled on the date of publication of the present volume; the information provided here may change. Be aware that many organizations take several weeks or longer to respond to inquiries, so allow as much time as possible.

Bullying.org

e-mail: help@bullying.org
website: www.bullying.org

Bullying.org is a website dedicated to raising awareness about the problem of bullying; educating youth, parents, and educators about how to address this problem; and working in cooperation with other stakeholders and organizations fighting bullying. The website provides extensive resources about the bullying problem, firsthand accounts of individuals who have dealt with bullying, and ways to help fight bullying.

Common Sense Media

650 Townsend, Suite 435
San Francisco, CA 94103
(415) 863-0600 • fax (415) 863-0601
website: www.commonsensemedia.org

Common Sense Media is an organization striving to ensure that youths' use of new media and technology does not have a negative effect on their social, emotional, and physical development. While much of the organization's focus centers on review and recommendation of movies and applications, the organization has also addressed cyberbullying. Articles such as "Stand Up to

Cyberbullying," videos covering cyberbullying prevention tips, and firsthand accounts of cyberbullying problems can be found on the website.

Gay, Lesbian and Straight Education Network (GLSEN)
(212) 727-0135
e-mail: glsen@glsen.org
website: www.glsen.org

GLSEN operates numerous chapters across the country to help ensure that lesbian, gay, bisexual, and transgender (LGBT) students have the opportunity to receive an education without fear of bullying or discrimination. The organization researches the bullying problem faced by LGBT students to help develop approaches and resources to address the issue, partners with outside individuals who can help enact solutions, and provides students with methods of making change in their own schools and communities. Information about all these activities can be found on the organization's website.

Girlshealth.gov
Department of Health and Human Services
200 Independence Avenue, SW, Room 712E
Washington, DC 20201
website: www.girlshealth.gov

Girlshealth.gov is a website maintained by the Office on Women's Health with the intent of providing reliable and accurate information on health issues specific to young women. Topics on the site include bullying, body, drugs, alcohol, smoking, and relationships. With regard to bullying, the website discusses cyberbullying, the unique ways that girls experience bullying, and how girls can address bullying themselves.

Great Schools
160 Spear Street, Suite 1020

San Francisco, CA 94105
website: www.greatschools.org

Great Schools has worked for fifteen years to provide information about schools' performance across the country with the hopes of providing parents with the necessary details to choose the appropriate schools for their children. The organization also focuses on many school-related issues, including bullying. Articles such as "Bullying: What You Can Do," "How They Do It in Finland," and "Don't Just Stand There" can all be accessed on the organization's website.

International Bullying Prevention Association (IBPA)

PO Box 99217
Troy, MI 28099
(800) 929-0397
e-mail: ibpainfo@stopybullyingworld.org
website: www.stopbullyingworld.org

IBPA is an international organization dedicated to promoting bullying prevention and policies based on sound research to create safer schools, improve work environments, and advance society. IBPA sponsors conferences to foster discussion about the problem of bullying and provides resources on its website for educators, parents, teens, and kids. These resources link to Stopbullying.gov and offer each of these groups' suggestions on ways that they can get involved and stop bullying.

National Crime Prevention Council (NCPC)

2001 Jefferson Davis Highway, Suite 901
Arlington, VA 22202
(202) 466-6272 • fax (202) 296-1356
website: www.ncpc.org

NCPC is a national organization seeking to help communities develop local methods of crime prevention using tools developed by the organization in combination with assistance from local crime enforcement agencies. Resources on bullying and cyberbullying can be found on the organization's website, including "Positive Change Through Policy" and cyberbullying podcasts.

PACER's National Bullying Prevention Center

8161 Normandale Boulevard
Bloomington, MN 55437
(888) 248-0822 • fax: (952) 838-0199
e-mail: bullying411@pacer.org
website: www.pacer.org/bullying

PACER's National Bullying Prevention Center has worked since its founding in 2006 to help communities find new, effective, and interactive methods to address bullying. It has created websites directed specifically to teens (PACERTeensAgainstBullying.org) and seeks to advance prevention efforts nationwide with PACER's National Bullying Prevention Month every October. PACER's bullying-prevention website provides videos about bullying, stories of individuals who face bullying, and resources with facts and research about bullying.

Stomp Out Bullying

www.stompoutbullying.org

Stomp Out Bullying is an organization founded by Love Our Children USA seeking to prevent bullying through programs such as its Annual Blue Shirt Day World Day of Bullying Prevention and its celebrity public service announcements that highlight the problem of bullying. Its website provides information on how teens who are being bullied can get help, how they can join the fight against bullying, and information about recent bullying initiatives in the news.

Stopbullying.gov

US Department of Health & Human Services
200 Independence Avenue, SW

Washington, DC 20201
website: www.stopbullying.gov

Stopbullying.gov is a website created as a central point where multiple government agencies can post information about the definitions of bullying and cyberbullying, who is affected by bullying, and what can be done to stop bullying. Specific prevention topics include "How to Talk About Bullying," "Prevention at School," "Working in the Community," and the "Bullying Prevention Training Center." Additionally, the website offers contact information for individuals who need help stemming from problems associated with bullying.

For Further Reading

Books

William Ayers, Bernadine Dohrn, and Rick Ayers, eds., *Zero Tolerance: Resisting the Drive for Punishment in Our Schools.* New York: New Press, 2001.

Emily Bazelon, *Sticks and Stones: Defeating the Culture of Bullying and Rediscovering the Power of Character and Empathy.* New York: Random House, 2013.

Kate Bornstein, *Hello Cruel World: 101 Alternatives to Suicide for Teens, Freaks and Other Outlaws.* New York: Seven Stories, 2006.

Barbara Coloroso, *The Bully, the Bullied, and the Bystander: From Preschool to High School—How Parents and Teachers Can Help Break the Cycle.* New York: HarperCollins, 2008.

Megan Kelley Hall and Carrie Jones, eds., *Dear Bully: Seventy Authors Tell Their Stories.* New York: HarperTeen, 2011.

Sameer Hinduja and Justin W. Patchin, *Bullying Beyond the Schoolyard: Preventing and Responding to Cyberbullying.* Thousand Oaks, CA: Corwin, 2009.

Thomas A. Jacobs, *Teen Cyberbullying Investigated: Where Do Your Rights End and Consequences Begin?* Minneapolis: Free Spirit, 2010.

Jessie Klein, *The Bully Society: School Shootings and the Crisis of Bullying in America's Schools.* New York: New York University Press, 2012.

Robin M. Kowalski, Susan P. Limber, and Patricia W. Agatston, *Cyberbullying: Bullying in the Digital Age.* Malden, MA: Wiley-Blackwell, 2012.

Lester L. Laminack and Reba M. Wadsworth, *Bullying Hurts: Teaching Kindness Through Read Alouds and Guided Conversations.* Portsmouth, NH: Heinemann, 2012.

Stephanie H. Meyer et al., eds., *Bullying Under Attack: True Stories Written by Teen Victims, Bullies and Bystanders.* Deerfield Beach, FL: Health Communications, 2013.

Dan Olweus, *Bullying at School: What We Know and What We Can Do.* Malden, MA: Blackwell, 1993.

Walter R. Roberts, *Bullying From Both Sides: Strategic Interventions for Working With Bullies and Victims.* Thousand Oaks, CA: Corwin, 2005.

Rachel Simmons, *Odd Girl Out: The Hidden Culture of Aggression in Girls.* New York: Mariner, 2011.

Periodicals

Jessica Bennett, "From Lockers to Lockup," *Newsweek,* October 11, 2010.

Mary Kate Cary, "Let's Quit Bullying Each Other, Please," *U.S. News Digital Weekly,* October 8, 2010.

John Cloud, "The Myths of Bullying," *Time,* March 12, 2012.

J. Dalton Courson and Abigayle C. Farris, "Title IX Liability for Anti-Gay Bullying," *Children's Rights Litigation,* Spring 2012.

Stan Davis and Charisse Nixon, "What Students Say About Bullying," *Educational Leadership,* September 2011.

Todd A. DeMitchell, "Bullying and the Conundrum of Free Speech in the United States," *Education and Law Journal,* August 2011.

Hilary Emery, "We Must Trust in Values to Vanquish Bullying," *Children and Young People Now,* November 13, 2012.

Bernie Froese-Germain, "Bullying Gets Digital Shot-in-the-Arm," *Education Canada,* Fall 2008.

Ameena K. Jandali, "Muslim Students in Post-9/11 Classrooms," *School Administrator,* October 2012.

Carmen Morais, "Bullies Behind Bars?," *Choices,* October 2012.

Susan Porter, "Why Our Approach to Bullying Is Bad for Kids," *Independent School,* Winter 2013.

Victor Rivero, "The Politicization of Bullying," *District Administration,* January 2011.

Bridget Roberts-Pittman, Julie Slavens, and Bradley V. Balch, "The Basics of Cyberbullying," *School Administrator*, April 2012.

Deborah Skolnik, "Bully Backlash," *Parenting School Years,* March 2013.

Emma Teitel, "Bullying 2.0 Is More like a Drama Class," *Maclean's,* October 17, 2011.

Kayla Webley, "A Separate Peace?," *Time,* October 24, 2011.

Index